Praise for Milt Allen's
Music, Artistry and Education:
A Journey Towards Musical Growth and Enlightenment

"It's truly a unique book in both its messages and its delivery. The stories absolutely relate the kinds of experiences that all of us have, but Milt has managed to find the hidden messages in these every day events. I can't think of another text that is so immediately accessible to the reader and flows so seamlessly into related concepts in our field, complete with specific suggestions for ways to improve our programs."

> — **Dr. Andrew Boysen,** Director of Bands, University of
> New Hampshire

"Thoughtful and inspiring. About being a musician and being human. It'll truly make you laugh and cry, and find the place where your talents and your desires meet. These kindly stories help us take a new look at ourselves, and a few of the 'sacred cows' and 'elephants' in our rehearsal rooms. A great read, with crackling wit and deep humanity."

> — **Larry Daehn,** Composer, President, Daehn Publications

"*Music, Artistry and Education* should be required reading for all conductors, at every stage of their musical lives. With devastating honesty and profound insight, Dr. Milton Allen compels us to step away from the 'business' of our lives and focus again on the art of our profession. Revealing personal examples ranging from humor to tragedy, Dr. Allen has created a stimulating and powerful blueprint for 'composing a life'—a unique and enormously valuable tool for every conductor."

> — **JoAnn Falletta,** Music Director, Buffalo Philharmonic Orchestra,
> Music Director, Virginia Symphony Orchestra, Member, National
> Council on the Arts, 2-time Grammy Winner

"Many years ago, my first Chinese conducting student taught me an invaluable lesson: 'when the student is ready, the teacher appears.' If you are a music educator primed to deepen as a musician and teacher, Milt Allen may prove to be just the teacher you seek! *Music, Artistry and Education: A Journey Towards Musical Growth and Enlightenment*, comprises down-to-earth stories, chock-full of meaningful lessons about music making, teaching, and life. In a world overrun with information, true wisdom has become a rare commodity. Allen's humorous and engaging stories contain a much-needed dose of this uncommon substance, serving to remind those of us who teach music of the things that matter most."

> — **Gary W. Hill,** Evelyn Smith Professor of Music, Director of
> Ensemble Studies, School of Music, Herberger Institute of Design
> and the Arts, Arizona State University

"Milt Allen has created a narrative about life, artistry, and teaching that is unlike anything that has come to us before. Consisting of eighteen homespun stories and both a prologue and an epilogue, this is a journey that has more depth and breadth than meets the eye upon a first read-through. This is a must read for teachers just entering the profession, for those teachers who have devoted many years of their life to sharing their love of music with others, and for everyone else between. The lens of understanding and revelation in subsequent re-reads, I suspect, will continue to evolve as the years of experience accumulate. Enjoy the journey, and take it often!"

> — **Craig Kirchhoff,** Director of Bands, Professor of Conducting, University of Minnesota

"We've heard of the need to 'sharpen the saw'. Well, Milt has provided a SHARPENER! For those of us crazy enough to make a life in music and music education, this book is a mirror, a map and a spark plug. Practical, personal, and inspirational, this is a book to return to like a favorite piece, uncovering new insights with every read."

> — **Lance LaDuke,** Trombone/Euphonium, Boston Brass

"*Music, Artistry and Education,* is a wonderful contribution to every music teacher's library, and—arguably—in every teacher's library. Being a Dr. Milt Allen fan, it is tempting to simply put together a string of positive accolades in support of the book's content, but—in this case—there is more written between the lines than on the lines, and that is always the mark of a masterful author. Dr. Allen has wrapped his creative pen around the real situational landscape of the music teaching/learning environment. He delightfully integrates his thought-and-experiences in a palatable style, and his gentle-and-priceless wisdom reveals, in story form, the key ingredients evidenced in every successful educator. Milt's book is one of those special contributions you will want to read, and reread, and reread again. Much like great music, it gets better with each performance/reading. You will find yourself 'nodding in agreement' as you flip from one page to the next, and with an uncontrollable smile you will realize Dr. Allen is a man who has traversed his own successful journey dealing with the challenges we all embrace along our own pathway. I applaud my colleague-and-friend for offering his message in such a wonderful fashion as he reminds of the critical role we play in the lives of our students. Thank you, my friend. Once again, you have made a grand difference for all of us."

> — **Dr. Tim Lautzenheiser,** Vice President of Education, Conn-Selmer, Inc

"Milt Allen has proven himself to be a powerfully effective music educator with students of all ages. Through *Music, Artistry and Education* he shares not only his deeply held thoughts on music education, but his distinctive take on *why* we do what we do. This series of attractive vignettes will inspire you to reassess your own educational philosophy and provide motivation toward infusing true creativity and artistic integrity into your teaching and music making."

— **Dr. Russel C. Mikkelson**, Professor, Director of Bands, The Ohio State University

"In the time I've known Milt Allen, I've observed him teach countless students and professionals about music and the music-making process. This book shows why they all come away understanding our art and themselves better. It reflects his humor, wisdom, compassion for people, and his passion for music and gives us all something deeper to focus on as we seek to become better musicians and people."

— **Doug Monroe**, Assistant Professor of Clarinet, North Dakota State University, Former Commander/Conductor, USAF Heritage of America Band

"*When you're up to your neck in alligators, it's tough to remember your initial objective was to drain the swamp.*

Milt Allen's wonderfully thought-provoking book deals with the A to Z of how to drain the swamp and how to cope with the alligators in life and in the music class room, drawing on experiences of a lifetime with real wit. He is certainly one of the funniest communicators in music education that I know. I remember with affection a lecture at a summer school in UK which had some thirty of us howling with laughter, not so much at what he said but the wonderfully disarming way in which he said it. Everything is grist for his mill, whether it is a rodeo with dog-riding monkeys, early life on the farm in the rural Midwest, climbing sand dunes with a small son in the Indiana Dunes National Lakeshore, learning to drive the hard way and so on, and each story ends with theories drawn and questions asked which will help any of us to tackle matters of study, of organization and rehearsal, and indeed of life, matters which we probably have taken for granted for years.

The gentle self-deprecating humour shines out from every page. Brimful of confidence, he faces the Eastman Wind Ensemble, knowing that he could 'read a score AND correct: pitch, balance, posture, articulation dynamics, tempos, accidentals, time signatures, wrong notes, entrances, exits, rhythms and sell enough candy bars to take a trip that, in doing so, would substantiate the value of music education to my parents, my administration, and, most importantly, ME'.

'Maestro Fennell, do you have any suggestions?' Time slowed, air stopped and the world stopped spinning for a moment. He looked at me and he said, waving his infinitely gifted right hand towards THE ensemble; 'Well, don't screw this up'.

This is a book to put on your bedside table, but the danger is you won't get much sleep, you will be led on through chapter after chapter of what I guess might be called 'homespun philosophy', beliefs and values derived from a wide range of experiences which will help anyone to become a better musician, educator and person."

— **Timothy Reynish**, Conductor, International Chamber Music Studio, Royal Northern College of Music, United Kingdom

"Milton Allen has written no ordinary book for band and orchestra conductors. It is, however, both funny and sad, naïve and deep, simple and profound, moving and poignant. While this is not a 'how-to' book, it is more unique and essential for the music educator than any other book about the profession I know. Filled with personal memories and lessons, Dr. Allen has a gift for writing as well as wonderful insights into the center of our humanistic selves. Easy reading along with deep reflections."

> — **H. Robert Reynolds,** Principal Wind Ensemble Conductor,
> The H. Robert Reynolds Professor of Music, Thornton School of
> Music, The University of Southern California

"Milton Allen's combination of sincerity, hilarity, and extensive career experience results in a rare and brilliant set of life lessons for the musically afflicted. In addition to Allen's inspired approach to fostering artistic truth, he teaches us that perhaps the most important skill a musician needs is a sense of humor."

> — **Alex Shapiro**, Award-winning composer

"Milton Allen's book is quite remarkable. Like most great educators he relates his subject, music education, to wonderful stories of everyday life. He is a wonderful storyteller and the connections are fascinating and at times revelatory. He is a friendly philosopher who deals with the theoretical and the practical while realizing that in the end it is about the music, and is pragmatic without losing sight of the artistic. This marvelous book should be read by all of us who in some way think of ourselves as teachers."

> — **Gerard Schwarz** Music Director, Seattle Symphony, 2-time Emmy
> Winner

Music, Artistry, AND Education

A Journey Towards
Musical Growth
and Enlightenment

MILTON ALLEN

Published by
Meredith Music Publications
a division of G.W. Music, Inc.
4899 Lerch Creek Ct., Galesville, MD 20765
http://www.meredithmusic.com

MEREDITH MUSIC PUBLICATIONS and its stylized double M logo are trademarks of
MEREDITH MUSIC PUBLICATIONS, a division of G.W. Music, Inc.

Cover and text design: Shawn Girsberger

International Standard Book Number: 978-1-57463-117-3
Cataloging-in-Publication Data is on file with the Library of Congress.
Library of Congress Control Number: 2011935074
Printed and bound in U.S.A.

Dedicated to the Phoenix in us all.

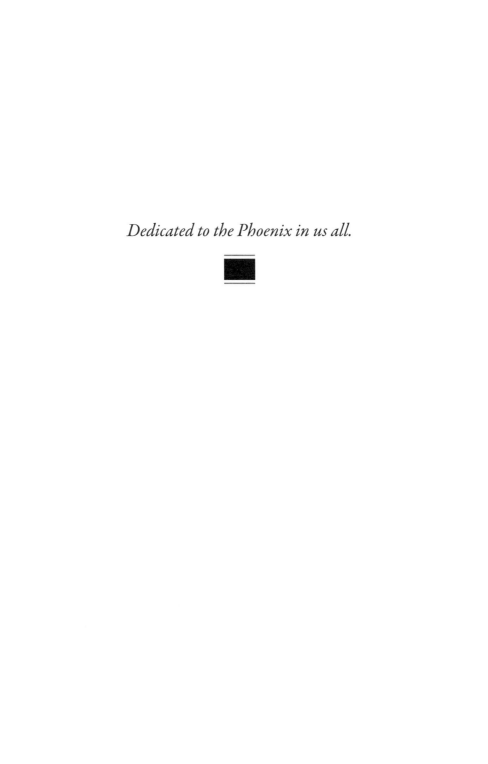

Contents

FOREWORD

If you've had the occasion to meet Milt Allen, you learn rather quickly that the man sees the world a bit differently than most. He invited me recently to his campus and it was my first extended dose of "the world according to Milt." I enjoyed an invigorating few days of great music making and stimulating discussion, but more importantly, I had the chance to bask in the glow of Milt Allen's optimism, wisdom, and humor. It was a delightful experience and I came away thinking that this guy was getting it all figured out, and that I wished I were as far along that same path.

It came as no surprise to me that Milt has found a means to share his informed outlook on life, art, and the world of teaching and conducting with a broader audience. This book lives up to its subtitle, "A journey towards musical growth and enlightenment." Through a series of stories, Milt draws upon the events of his life that have shaped his thinking and nourished his soul to lead the readers to signposts—his benevolent, suggested calls to action that the reader might employ in order to stimulate personal exploration. Now this guy is a great writer! I must admit I was a bit surprised at just how good Milt was at pulling me into the moment described in each story. I literally laughed out loud a few times—most of the stories are shared with a self-depre-cating flair. There are other stories that grow from the more troubling moments Milt experienced, and these have a rather profound weight to them. All of the stories seemed to resonate easily with the arc of my teaching life, and I would think other educators would find readily a similar connection. Milt draws you into a scenario with wonderfully descriptive prose, and then with the gentle hand of a master teacher, points out what he learned from each. He shares his life lessons as sign-posts, launching them as calls to action and reflection. I found myself eager to take the time to ponder and let them in, and I grew. I was thankful that he took the time to help me out.

With his new book, Milt has given us a personal gift of lasting value. I heartily recommend it to any teacher who needs to come up for air, let alone those who are just getting ready to dive into the water for the first time.

Dr. Timothy Mahr
Professor of Music
Conductor, St. Olaf Band
Composer

ACKNOWLEDGEMENTS

You know, it's kinda funny. We've all read those "acknowledgement" sections before books we've read and maybe dreamt, "If I ever got the opportunity . . . " And now, here I am with that opportunity and I realize I can't begin to adequately convey to all the people all the thanks they deserve. My mental hard drive crashes just trying to retrieve the names of those who have helped me to the place I am now. With that said, I'll give it a try, but, please, feel free to add your name to the list. I certainly mean no disrespect!

To my wife Margaret, son Benjamin, and daughter Madeline, for their patience and support for much longer than it should have been needed.

To Denny Senseney and Tim Lautzenheiser, whose support, belief, and counsel helped get this project off the ground.

To Russ Mikkelson for shared beliefs and the resolve therein.

To every gall-dang student I've ever had. Really.

To Bob Marshall for his direction early in the project. I only wish he was still here to see its fruition.

To Susan Gedutis Lindsay, who proved to me the value of clarity in writing.

To Shawn Girsberger for her artistry with regard to the visual sense of the written word.

To Gar Whaley for serving as an example of belief, patience, insight, and understanding. Of course, expertise is understood! Also, for allowing me to not only retain my overall vision of this work, but to help illuminate it.

To music: I can never thank you enough . . . But thanks.

And to Mr. Gayle McMillen: Thanks. You made a difference in my life.

PREFACE

Stories link us. A common, shared experience can help us along our individual journeys through life. Through stories, we can find comfort in the knowledge that others have passed this way before. Through stories, we can learn lessons that might shape our lives in some way. In fact, all encounters and events in our life, no matter how small, can become our teachers, if we choose to seek their wisdom.

The true stories and reflections that follow are personal. They have shaped me, as a musician, music educator, and conductor, and I offer them to you in the hopes that you might benefit even from my follies. It's not easy to share some of these stories, but I do so because each can contain a deeper truth for any of us, depending on our own individual paths. I encourage you to read them and re-read them, both in the near future and in the years to come as your experiences change. Perhaps a new meaning may be gleaned.

Finally, these stories are offered in the spirit of simplicity. They are easily read and as such designed for deeper contemplation. It is my hope that they will inspire you on your artistic journey, contemplating those things that you have experienced in your own life, with an open mind and heart for those lessons you may have yet to truly discover.

Prologue. Dog-Ridin' Monkeys

Remember? Remember that first moment? That first moment when you absolutely *knew* that music had to be an important part of your life? For some of us, that memory might seem like yesterday. For others of us, though, it could very well be something lost in the day-to-day of a life in music. It's a paradox, isn't it? Kind of like the old quip: "When you're up to your neck in alligators, it's tough to remember your initial objective was to drain the swamp!"

Dog-ridin' monkeys. Yes, I just wrote "dog-ridin' monkeys" in a book whose main subject matter is music. It was at a rodeo in Oklahoma City when I first saw that unlikely spectacle: Monkeys atop small dogs that were taking them every which way imaginable in an effort to herd sheep in a small corral. Let me assure you that this blurred explosion of fur and wool truly defies description. Suffice to say that it results, amazingly, with all sheep in the corral.

That's when I had a moment of educational epiphany: I, as a music educator, am that monkey, and perhaps you are one too. Those sheep are my musicians, and the corral is musically where I want to get them. And the dog? That dog is my rehearsal, my day, my family, my obligations, dreams, and expectations—in short, all the things that make up my musical life and that affect the life and learning of those around me. Sometimes I can control the dog; sometimes I can't. Either way, the question is: How can I stay focused on the "sheep" and successfully get them into the "corral?" And that, friends, is a rub, ain't it?

Maybe that is not the most important question, though. An even more important question is: How do we continue to develop *ourselves* as music artist/educators while we work with our sheep? How do we continue to musically evolve, reaching the understanding of a Fennel, Reynolds, Paynter, Battisti, Revelli, Hunsberger, Kirchhoff, Croft, Whitwell, Corporon, Junkin, Mikkelson, Haithcock, Hill, and the myriad of conductors I've just offended by not listing?

This is a tough one for any of us in this artful vocation. An old grizzled character named Curly philosophizes in the 1991 movie *City Slickers* that the most important thing in life is that "one thing." The characters spend the rest of the movie searching for the answer to Curly's simple piece of advice, analyzing and picking apart the meaning of his statement, and in so doing, missing the big picture. Still not quite clear? Think of your rehearsal. Are you focusing on smaller things, never getting to the big picture?

I was fortunate to have in my life several Curly characters, who reminded me to focus on the big picture. One in particular was my first assistant superintendent in charge of the arts program for the school district. In fact, this guy could probably whip Curly in a fair fight. He was passionate about his beliefs and the importance of music in everyone's lives and it was his passion that helped me along the path toward developing my philosophies of both music and education. Over twenty years later, he still takes up residence in my soul's practice room.

I spent seventeen years teaching in public and parochial schools in both urban and rural settings large and small. I was then kidnapped and taken to the "Ivory Tower" of the university setting, where I have spent the years since, having taught in both small and large institutional settings. As a result, some may now regard me as a university conductor whose pure, noble pursuit of art prevents me from understanding what is *really* happening in music and education. I sit in my office smoking a pipe, they surmise, reading classic poetry, examining new scores to perform with my exceptional students, and pondering great things, venturing out only to either rehearse my impeccable group or to offer a rare photo-op with those lucky enough to be in my presence. Others may regard me as a music educator directly from the trenches, wearing the sheepskin of a university professor. According to them, I don't really understand art—in fact, I didn't know you had to spell it with the letter "a" before the sound "rt." I focus only on notes and rhythms and am incapable of gleaning greater artistic meaning. I conduct like a windmill detached from its spindle and I am constantly asking for an extra-duty contract to begin an after-school detention program at the university level.

Perhaps I am a bit harsh toward my conjured critics, but my experience has led me to believe that our musical landscape is headed for trouble if we each don't begin to find that "one thing" again. Perhaps our pursuit of it should start with that question I asked at the beginning of this prologue: Remember? Do you remember why you chose music in the first place, and are you guided by that vision in your day-to-day teaching and/or performing experiences?

This book is designed to not only help you remember, but to help you along your own artistic path based on that vision. It is a collection of stories that offer a combination of practical, theoretical, and philo-sophical guidance on the art of music teaching and performance. The experiences relayed are gleaned from my own journey, and also from those who have mentored me along the way. At the end of most of these observations are "signposts" that identify a "what," "when," and "how," in order to guide you as you apply a specific concept taken from the story to your own musical journey. I would also like to encour-age you to record the answers to some of the questions asked, or any thoughts are ideas that might come to you. You never know when those moments of epiphany will happen and it would be a shame to lose even one of them!

The exercises, suggestions, and challenges presented in this book are designed to help take you further along in your personal path of musical growth and/or enlightenment. This path is different for all of us, and that "one thing" Curly advises us to seek will be unique for each of us. Your journey will be uniquely yours, but we all begin from the same point: by spending some time to remember . . .

Silent Conversations

I was born and raised in Kansas. Like most kids, I thought anywhere else was surely better than where I was. I was always thinking about trying to get over that rainbow to see something different. My parents came from poor backgrounds. My dad was the third of five rural children and my mom was the first of five. Neither was a musician, although my dad likes to kid me about being the leader of the White City, Kansas Stick Rhythm Band in eighth grade. Neither had a college education, so thankfully they did not have to face the possibility of being educated beyond their intelligence, as I was. They were, as Dad puts it, from the "College of Hard Knocks," whose proud colors were black and blue. Tough and practical, they raised their four children to be the same. A strong work ethic was always of paramount value.

When my two sisters were in high school, my dad would encourage them to invite boyfriends over for Sunday dinner. Initially, all involved would take the bait. However, everyone soon realized that these invitations served very distinct purposes:

- a home-cooked meal for said guests,
- a chance for said guests to meet the family,
- a chance for Dad to size up these young men, most readily by

- saving the largest job of our little ten-acre place for those days when a few extra hands were required, thereby
- enabling my father to judge the work ethic of said individuals.

Pretty smart—in fact, brilliant—use of personnel and time management.

Now, one must consider the importance of keen observation here. We learn a lot about others without words. The whole "actions speak louder than words" thing, I find, is absolutely accurate. Having the skill to watch, or better yet *listen,* instead of speak can help in almost any situation. Jimi Hendrix once said, "Knowledge speaks, but wisdom listens." Go Jimi. In my experience, I have more frequently observed this ability to listen in the company of people who have calloused hands and sun-worn creases around their smiles. It is they who have developed a quiet resolve and solid work ethic through the trials of simply making ends meet through a life in the field. I have observed the greatest wisdom while standing with them at a fence post amid the ringing loudness of a silent conversation.

Watching the sun. Watching the crops. Watching the cattle. Watching the world go by. Let's face it, it can be easy to ridicule the rural Midwesterner, but the stereotype of Midwestern conversation—leaning against a fence post and grunting every fifteen to twenty minutes—can be, well, fairly accurate. And there's absolutely nothing wrong with that. Do you know why? Because it isn't about the words—it's about the common observation and its sublime impact on those observing. And when words are spoken, they are carefully chosen for their brevity, familiarity, and clarity.

When we are in front of an ensemble, I believe it is no different. We must invite others into the process of making music—not force them. It is then that we can begin to discern what needs to be done and how those wonderful souls before us can be encouraged to do it. We must "listen" with eyes wide open and "see" with our ears. As the ones who drew the short straw and stand in front, we must bring the group, as a whole, to "hear" a common observation and to embrace it. And, of course, we must be respectful enough to carefully choose our words with brevity, familiarity, and clarity. In short, we must lead as though leaning on that fence post, helping all to bask in the sun of that common musical observation.

SIGNPOSTS

What:

Create an inviting and collaborative rehearsal environment where education and art take place. This environment should be conducive to each ensemble member listening to and hearing each other, and taking an active part in the music-making process.

When:

The beginning of a semester, quarter, or rehearsal sequence *or* one rehearsal prior to when you would like to initiate this environment.

How:

1. Be sure to begin rehearsal with *silence*—many students aren't used to this and it can be uncomfortable for them!

- Distinguish between practice and rehearsal. Remind students that practice is what a musician does individually to learn the part; rehearsal is where a musician comes to learn ***everyone else's part.***

- Tell your students that you understand that their day can be quite hectic and noisy, and remind them that now, "We get to make *music*." Explain that the silence is intended to help create an appropriate environment— a moment to "clear the haze" out of their heads, a bit of time where the "I" can become a "we" focused on being *in* the moment. Let them know that, tomorrow, we are going to . . .

- Establish five to ten seconds before *any* sound or instruction is given. We will begin to create the moment!

- If someone is talking or moving, simply look at them in an inviting way—don't scold! In fact, smile! No "mean" looks!

2. Once this silence is established, continue to build on this mutual trust during rehearsal with supportive comments—find the *good* in what's happening. Acknowledge musicians' efforts and then guide them toward what you want to hear. Statements like, "That's WRONG" or "Don't do it like that" are not appropriate. We want to believe that the musicians under our charge are trying to perform as we would like, but just need a bit more guidance or input (not necessarily from you). Statements like, "That's it, now; could you make it even shorter?" not only acknowledge

our musician's efforts, but create an environment of collaboration rather than dictation.

3. Change the perspective by involving *everyone*! Remember: Mutual trust is essential in this process, but especially the ensemble's trust in *you*! Try:

    - **Silent rehearsal**. Not a word from you. You may use anything at your disposal to teach, e.g. gesture, board, paper, visual aid, etc., but do not use your voice: only eyes and ears. Try this for five minutes the first time, then, gradually extend the time!

    - **Festival seating**: Musicians may sit/stand anywhere they want within the present chair configuration and with the following guidelines:

        - (Band or orchestra) Percussion must stay put!

        - Musicians may not sit/stand beside anyone in their section (if at all possible), unless a folder must be shared.

Either play through a piece *or* rehearse it. After a while, have the students move back into their original position. (Allowing sixty seconds to make the changes prevents excessive loss of rehearsal time.) Ask if anyone heard anything they had not heard before. (Be ready for almost every hand to go up.) Then, begin rehearsing the same piece again, stressing that musicians need to be able to hear the parts they just heard for possibly the first time—awareness and balance are key!

    - **Chamber seating**. Musicians sit/stand in circles of quartets/quintets throughout the room. It is essential that no one play the same instrument/part in each "chamber group." The rules:

- ■ The conductor counts off the piece, *but does not conduct it.*

- ■ When a musician hears something that they feel is either incorrect or can be done better, they raise their hand. The conductor stops the ensemble.

- ■ The musician must cite the specific problem as a challenge, and then *provide a possible solution.* (This is not a gripe session designed to fan egos.)

- ■ Conductor then counts off piece again.

- **Blind rehearsal/conductor-less rehearsal.** Either the ensemble performs without a conductor or the lights are turned off in the rehearsal room. The rules:

  - ■ If the lights are on, students may take physical cues but ultimately must rely completely on the ability to recognize not only their musical "place" in the piece, but what, at any given time, their role is. The conductor simply monitors and stops the ensemble when an improvement needs to take place or to get ensemble feedback.

  - ■ If the lights are off, students will need to have the music memorized—a routinely used warm-up chorale is a great way to start—and then rely completely on what is heard. The conductor can use a flashlight to signal when to stop and proceed, as indicated above.

Additional thoughts:

- Trust is *key* for all of these suggestions—work in "baby steps."
- Don't impose. Include! Change imposed is change opposed.
- Enable! Allow the students to take part by supporting *positive* participation.

WEBS

I really enjoy the outdoors. I do a lot of running and biking when I can and always seem to learn something when I go out. Since the running occupies my conscious mind, it allows my subconscious thoughts to really "Grainger": come to the fore! As a result, some of my best thinking comes when I'm outdoors, basking in alpha waves and enjoying what nature's rehearsal room has to offer.

One hot summer morning I went on a run in the woods in a state park near my home. It's a nice run and its challenges include short, lung-busting climbs, tramping through thick grassy trails, and dancing over tangled roots. When you run in the woods in the morning, you can't be too skittish about spiders and webs. Evening is a prime feasting time for our little eight-legged brothers and you can bet that you will run through webs stretched between branches across open trails. Every time I do this, I think of Gary Larsen's *Far Side* cartoon depicting two spiders that have just completed weaving a web at the bottom of a playground slide. One spider remarks to the other: "If we pull this off, we'll eat like kings!"

On this particular morning, I seemed to be running into more than my share of webs . . . an *unusually generous* share of webs. It became a little disconcerting, as it seemed to indicate that I was venturing well off the beaten path. I began to envision Indiana Jones in *Raiders of the Lost Ark* as he first entered the cave at the beginning of the movie. Then, as synapses would have it, *Arachnophobia*. Of course, all the pictures I had ever seen of spider bites began to come to mind, too. It was both damp and shadowy where I was running and it became difficult to tell whether it was an embalmed little package that whacked my face and upper body, or if it was indeed Charlotte's evil cousin. I wiped away the sticky muck as fast as I could, at times doing that little out-of-control, "I'm freaking out" rapid-hand-motion thing that seems to be some primal survival instinct. But, I pressed forward, resolute in completing not only my present course, but enjoying a beautiful morning of solitude. The webs ceased as the trail opened a bit, and as I was running, I noticed a sign coming up on my left. As a passed it, I glanced back and saw that it read: "Trail Closed." I had just run through an entire closed section of trail, which hadn't been marked at the other end.

I thought back as to why it was closed, because it was in fact the most beautiful portion of my run so far that morning. Despite the webs during one section, the terrain had offered a relaxing view alongside a river. Dense, green foliage with rays of sunlight shining through, two small creeks, wonderful twists and bends, scores of animal tracks, and a deer sighting were all a part of this closed trail. And the sounds! The symphony included frog choirs, assisted by chirping crickets, the gentle ostinato of the river, aleotoric hooves thrashing through the foliage, and the sporadic, bright crack of a heavy limb breaking under the pressure of just *being*. Birds would add their recitative to the musical tapestry and all the while my feet kept tempo on a music score of dirt, dust, and leaves. Had I turned back, I would never have experienced that particular movement of the morning's concert.

How often have we stopped at the webs—those things that would seem to indicate either a "wrong direction" or at least one in which few dared go? In the beginning of our music education careers, it is certainly wise to follow those wider, more established trails. We learn those trails as both a means of gaining knowledge as well as gaining a right of passage further into our profession. In addition, we also learn them in order to be able to blaze our own trail, to find a way that suits our particular musical self as well as teaching style. We all have those great artist educator/musicians who have influenced us and continue to do so.

We have all attended conferences and in-services where outstanding clinicians have offered their expertise regarding all things musical and educational. I think there are four basic reactions to these clinics:

1. "I can certainly use ideas from this."
2. "I already do those things, but now I'm reassured."
3. "I could have done that clinic, only better."
4. "That works for the clinician, but it won't work for me because (fill in the blank.)"

But these are just microcosms of the webs. When we break through those webs and blaze our own trails, when we see things objectively, we begin to realize that it's not just "Trail Closed," but "World Open." We see our own musical paths. We embrace our own teaching styles. We begin to see what we really are and can be on the podium. And, by doing so, we present to those in our musical charge a pure and passionate musical personification. We see that there is no one else who, at that moment, would be better suited to pass the essence of musical artistry to those in that rehearsal room, or to ourselves. Webs? Trail closed? World open.

SIGNPOSTS

What:

Embracing or further seeking *our* teaching/podium style.

When:

Today!

How:

1. Begin by videotaping yourself in rehearsal—this is the most objective evaluation tool that you can use.

2. Watch the recording, making objective observations. It is important that you make absolutely no subjective judgments at this time. Simply record what you see.

3. Think about what you just observed. Now, assume the role of master teacher. Go back and notate your observations as either:

    - strategies or gestures that worked, or
    - surprises that didn't work as well as you thought they did
    - Also note what you do well! These are areas you will definitely want to build on.

4. Go back through the list a second time and identify those things that appear to have been borrowed or learned from another source.

5. Make a determination as to whether those things:

    - truly worked
    - could work for you

- could work for you if modified
- won't work for you

6. Ask yourself: What do I think a master teacher would do? Try it! Take chances! Try something new! Finding out what doesn't work points you toward what does. Remember—you can always ask others to view that tape and offer suggestions, too.

7. Don't stop at rehearsal. Look at other aspects of your curriculum, administration, or entire program. Have you adapted your strengths—and what you can offer—to these aspects?

8. Embrace your strengths and knowledge of your program and mix it with not just what you've learned, but what you think might work. There is no one on this planet like you. Run through the "webs" and bring those in your rehearsal room the pure *you*!

Music for Prague and the Three Wise Men

S o there I was, standing in front of the Eastman Wind Ensemble as a conducting fellow for their fortieth anniversary celebration. Directly in front of me was the first movement of Karel Husa's incredible *Music for Prague*. Sitting on stage just to my right were E. Clyde Roller, Donald Hunsberger, and Frederick Fennell. They were staring at me. And I was staring back thinking: *What am I DOING here?*

I was in the middle of a master's program and had the great fortune and opportunity to participate in this historic occasion. I had taken a sabbatical from my position at the time, taking a year to help me become the greatest, most astounding, most celebrated conducting genius to ever grace the wind-band podium. Fast track, fast track, fast track—that's what I was about. Flash and dash. Being perceived as great with a capital "G" was the most important thing. I had no idea at the time that the *composer* might play some type of roll in all of this stuff, let alone the ensemble. As an individual of incredible and considerable experience—I had almost taught five whole years—I had all the answers and was still waiting to tell everyone.

Technique was everything. I had it figured out: If I looked good and pronounced words like "Milhaud" and "Lincolnshire" correctly, then the ensemble would be mesmerized and in so being, create one magical, musical moment after another. If they didn't, it sure wasn't my fault. Remember, I looked *good*. And I felt good pretending to be what I thought a conductor was, what a master teacher was.

In order to further enhance my artistry and be the first wind band–based conductor to enjoy a completely freelance career, I pursued a master's degree. Now, I think I did know a bit. And I did seek out answers, truly determined to better myself. I was very comfortable in front of an ensemble, or at least falsely confident. I could read a score *and* correct pitch, balance, posture, articulation, dynamics, tempos, accidentals, time signatures, wrong notes, entrances, exits, and rhythms—and sell enough candy bars to take my students on a band trip that would substantiate the value of music education to parents, administration, and, most importantly, ME. Yes sir: Put me in front of them Eastman folks and I'll a'learn'em somethin' 'bout the *musics!*

I wasn't afraid to ask anyone questions either, which led me to my brief exchange with Maestro Fennell himself, upon our first meeting on that stage at Eastman. Seeking to speak to Him and have an exchange that would be one for the ages, one that would capture the essence of all musical space and time, that would cause the heavens to part and angels to sing, providing me with years of "I remember what Maestro Fennell said to me," that would cause all to lean forward in their chairs in hushed silence, waiting for those gems of wisdom, I asked him: "Maestro Fennell, do you have any suggestions?" Time slowed, air stopped, and the world stood still for a moment. He looked up at me and he said, waving his infinitely gifted right hand toward *the* ensemble: "Well. Don't screw this up!"

Don't screw this up. DON'T SCREW THIS UP! I laughed a knowing laugh, a confident laugh. It was the kind of laugh that two musicians share when they sense far deeper musical truths. Those around laughed, too. Ahhh, such musical humor. I stepped to the podium in front of *the* ensemble. Suddenly, the realization set in: who was seated both in front of me and beside me, and the one person they were looking at. At that moment, the baton vibrato started in my left ankle. It jumped to the other ankle and proceeded up both legs. Fast. Really fast. It streaked through my upper torso, burned out my internal sweat-prevention apparatus, and finally shot through my arms to my hands.

Now, I thought I knew this dang "Hoosah" tune. I knew where the entrances were (kind of) and I could recognize rhythms from the score, just like I did with my bands back home. Course, that doesn't mean I could do it all at once. No problem; I would just listen for the wrong "stuff" and be my incredible self. The three wise men would exalt this young phenom, this Wunderkind, when I stepped off of the "stage." Bodda-bing-bodda-boom: instant career. I gave a downbeat—not a preparatory—just a downbeat. Kind of like a starter's pistol at the beginning of a 100-yard dash. They began to play. Oh man, did they begin to play. Oh MAN, DID THEY BEGIN TO PLAY!

I tried to follow. Really. I tried hard. I wanted to stop, except I had no idea where we were and couldn't make any kind of appropriate comment regarding what they were playing. So, I emoted. I rolled my eyes to the back of my head. I stabbed, slashed, poked, and pleaded. But most of all, I made a realization: I had absolutely *nothing* to say. Not just words, but *music*. Nothing. Nada. No-thing. They, apparently, had no problem with pitch, balance, posture, articulation, dynamics, tempos, accidentals, time signatures, wrong notes, entrances, exits, or rhythms. What would I bring to the equation? Up until that moment, I thought I knew what being a conductor was, what being a teacher was, what being a *musician* was. I was one of those guys who would hear great performances and think to myself, "Big deal. If I had those musicians, I could do that, too." Of course, this is looking at the ensemble as a self-contained, preformed unit that just simply *happens.*

Well, I tried very hard to rewrite that first movement beginning with the warning fanfare. But *the* ensemble chose, instead, to perform what was closer to the piece. In fact, some members graciously stopped me in the hallway later to tell me what a terrific job I had done. They later pursued careers as stunt-doubles for Pinocchio. Of course, everyone could see and feel my terror—how wonderful they were to make such comments. Perhaps Maestro Fennell summed it up best when he said, "Well, once again, very different, but very good." Next, please.

Sometimes when the boat is sinking, an escape hatch opens. As it was, this event did turn into a pivotal moment in my career, though not the one I had anticipated. As directors, we spend a lot of time in front of our ensembles covering pitch, balance, posture, articulation, dynamics, tempos, accidentals, time signatures, wrong notes, entrances, exits, rhythms . . . and selling candy. We listen for mistakes and take a reactive approach to creating Art. What I learned on that day is one of the most profound lessons I have ever learned. The lesson is this: If we stood in front of *the* ensemble and all of the aforementioned things were taken care—nothing to fix, so to speak—what would we have to offer?

Perhaps our teaching should start *there*—regardless of the level of the ensemble. We didn't join band or orchestra or choir to drill, did we? Well, our students didn't either. They joined because music is fun, because it moved them in some way, because others have fun doing it. Because it *is* what it *is* to each and every young musician. Who are we to dissect the essence of music under the guise of art? Because we can explain all the musculature and bone in the human arm doesn't mean that we understand its full potential and importance in the body as a whole. So, then, why do we sometimes deny our students (if we do) the larger musical picture? Why not treat and expect musical moments as if they were *the* ensemble—that is to say, any one of our outstanding universities, military, or other professional bands, orchestras, or choirs? Perhaps if we can, we not only show our ensembles a larger musical picture, but also release our musical souls for them to experience—those same souls that whispered to us to forge a musical life when we sat where our ensembles do now.

SIGNPOSTS

What:

Teaching beyond the "toolbox": guiding our ensembles toward a larger musical goal on a piece.

When:

The beginning of the rehearsal sequence for any piece.

How:

1. Start by raising your own rehearsal/performance benchmarks.

    -   Watch videos of *great* conductors (in rehearsal if possible).

    -   Listen to great recordings!

    -   Take a day and attend a rehearsal of a recognized conductor in (or out) of your geographical era.

    -   Take an active part in conducting symposia or events, which enable you to have hands-on experience.

    -   Seek out a person whom you respect and adopt him or her as your mentor!

    -   *Call the composer!* They rarely get calls and are often very eager to assist you in relaying what is important on "their" piece.

    -   The phone is one of the greatest teacher aids we have. Use it often!

2. Save development of the musical basics for the warm-up. Rehearsal proper should generally be dedicated toward the larger musical picture.

3. Be sure that suggestions are given within the context of the larger musical picture. Relate musical requests within that framework.

4. Involve the ensemble members through *inquiry*. Ask *them* the who, what, where, and why!

5. Remember the following question: Is the composer's intent being communicated to the audience? In other words, how

should the audience "react" to the performance of the piece? (Of course, this implies that the conductor has done the homework and has, in turn, established a vision with the ensemble!)

A View from the Ivory Tower: Climbing the Sand Dunes

The great outdoors! Since my wife and I wanted to both foster a love of the outdoors with our two small children, as well as start an annual family summer vacation tradition, we decided to begin with a visit to the Indiana Dunes National Lakeshore.

The dunes are located along Lake Michigan within sight—on a clear day—of the downtown Chicago skyline to the west. We readied ourselves for the adventure of the summer and drove the three and a half hours from our home in Illinois to our selected camping area. It was extremely hot that summer, but we knew that we had preselected a campsite with plenty of tree coverage to help keep our tent cool. What we didn't know was that the emerald ash borers had laid waste to that neck of the woods and every single tree in the campground had been cut. In addition, more camping "spots" had been added. So, what we ended up with was a campground that looked more like the caravans that used to follow the Grateful Dead, with people spilling over into each other's personal space, except where cut and splintered tree trunks remained. This, however, did not bother us in the least. We were going to go swimming and hiking! The campground would return to its former self in time as well, so all was good.

We pitched the tent as fast as we could and headed down to the water. We were reminded how hot sand can get in 100-degree heat, especially if you lose your sandals and you're five years old—at least I *felt* like I was five years old as I walked and reminisced of vacations when I was much, much, much younger. I discovered that having your feet on fire really detracts from your ability to reminisce. Or think. Or remain composed in front of your children. But we finally made it.

For two days we enjoyed the beach, followed by a bit of hiking and drives into the surrounding area. The beach was beautiful, fine-grained sand and the water was crystal clear. I would put on my straw hat and set my lawn chair down into about three to four feet of water and plant. This was a little bit of heaven. But there was one thing . . .

I noticed this one dune that reached up from the shore. It was the largest dune there and I was surprised that no one was trying to climb it. It sure didn't look that difficult and, by the third day, I figured I would just run up that sucker and take in what surely must be an incredible view from the top. So I struck out. My son asked me what I was up to and when I explained I was going to climb that dune, he decided that sounded pretty cool. So, along came the seven-year-old.

Strange what goes through your mind as you realize that you've committed to something you thought you had a pretty good understanding of at the beginning but, as it turns out, is far more challenging than originally anticipated. And others are watching every step you take.

The first few steps weren't so bad. Heck, I was even walking upright. But then, as I took a step forward, my foot sank almost eighteen inches into the dune, sliding back at the same time. It was like walking in a big, thick mud puddle that was on fire—so I couldn't leave my foot in the sand very long (despite wearing some very tight sandals). Of course, my son was right behind me, watching everything Dad was doing. What seemed like a short, gentle incline to the top of a relatively small dune now proved to be a steep incline up a dune that was easily one hundred-plus yards, composed of steps like the one I just took. As I began to slide backwards, I realized that I had to lunge three steps at a time, then stop for a break of about thirty seconds to allow my lungs to catch up in order to make any progress (three steps forward, two steps sliding back).

I was particularly surprised that I had to stop and take in oxygen, since I thought that I was in at least decent shape and prepared for the rigors of what the vacation may bring. This both scared me a bit and forced me to realize that I was really in for it. I decided that I wouldn't look up as much as I would look down. I found that the only sure way to measure distance was to see how far I'd come, not how far I had to go. Plus, I was able to monitor my son who, because of his lighter weight, was having a little bit of an easier time, but not much. And so it went, lungs burning, sweat dripping, son watching and following, but full of determination to reach the top.

Now, let's leave the boys to climb the dune for a moment and return to teaching. I remember when I first started teaching, I would hear incredible groups from other schools. The Midwest Clinic was chock-full of great ensembles, too. And, of course, college groups. Please, I mean, really. I thought, "Give me those players and I can get the same (if not better) results." Those folks waving their arms in front of those college bands and orchestras had to suck up something *huge* to get where they are, I thought, unless, of course, they knew the right people. Eventually, I felt compelled to teach at the collegiate level, driven by a desire to both have a more direct impact on future educators as well as to really focus on the art of performance without things like field trips, bus requests, and booster groups interfering. I didn't know it then, but I was in for a crash-course in the university learning curve.

The first lesson I learned at the university was this: There truly is never enough time. Ever. Until teaching at the university, it was as if I'd been raising bees in order to harvest fine wax that I would refine and mold into a candle—which I would then burn at both ends and the middle, accomplishing almost anything I set out to do in a relatively short time. Now, this was no longer the case. I discovered that time is one of our greatest commodities, whether in our personal or professional lives. Having enough time is not a case of making *more* time; it's really about taking the time we have to do what needs done.

I tend to look at time as money and I consider myself rich in time (since I'll never have much money). Now, how do I choose to spend it? On myself? Sometimes. On those projects that demand it? Yes. On family? Hello. On friends? Which brings up a good point: Time invested wisely can have great returns. What about time on our art? What about that score that contains all that buried musical treasure? More importantly, in keeping focus on our vocation, how are we using our musician's investment of time in us? How many of us have stayed just ahead of our ensemble's progress while at the same time, rehearsing a piece for, say, three months? Is that fair to those investing in us? And what could we be doing if we used that investment more wisely and frugally? Could we be offering more for the investment?

But back to that dune. Well, I was in the thick of it and there was no way I was going back down that dune. I lost myself in my trek, focusing all energy forward. Then, it happened. Shade. The shade afforded by the trees at the top of the dune. Within five minutes I was able to scale the last ten feet and look back. The view was incredible—not the one of the lake and all the surroundings, but of the speck that had come two-thirds of the way up the dune following me: my son. But, he had stopped. Knowing that I had made it, that I had experienced it, that I could maybe guide him and offer support, I shouted down to him. He looked up and saw me there. He saw me there . . . and began to move forward. It took a while, but with my support and his belief in me along with his determination, he made it.

We stood there for a moment, then after a hug, raised our hands in silent celebration. Both separately and together, we had stuck with it and accomplished something that we may carry with us for the rest of our lives—I know I will. The time invested reaped a harvest for both me and, I hope, my son. Maybe one day he will look back on this event with the benefit of a more mature observation.

But what of us—of you and me? How are we investing our time with our students? Are we simply cruising through classes, staying ahead just enough to make it through the next rehearsal? Are we teaching only to perfection or possibility? Or are we short-changing the capabilities of our students in return for musical safety following, as Russel Mikkelson puts it, the "path of least persistence?" And the Ivory Towers? What would you do if you were there, if you supposedly had the time and the students and the ensembles?

Why not start right now, wherever you are, with that perspective? Therein lie the possibilities and an investment that will reap benefits not just for you, but also for the next generation of artists you are creating. The artists whom we may forget are right behind us, watching everything we do, and waiting for us to help them "up" and show them "the way."

SIGNPOSTS

What:

Use of time—squeezing the possibilities.

When:

Time frames are given along with the suggestions found below under "How."

How:

1. Two weeks before a concert, choose one piece of music one to two grade levels below what you are programming on the concert. Add it to the program and begin rehearsing it within the current schedule. Perform it on that next concert without letting the audience know what you did—the members of the ensemble will know and that's what matters most. (They'll tell their parents anyway, but you don't want to openly elicit a false audience response merely for the effort. This is more toward a "professional" way of preparing anyway!)

2. Follow the same procedure as above, but with only one week before a performance. Perhaps this might be for the next concert.

3. In preparation for rehearsal, get a CD or MP3 player and play pieces related to either concepts you will teach or pieces on upcoming programs, as students enter the room. This will provide an anticipatory environment that will spring you and the ensemble into the rehearsal.

4. Be sure to post all rehearsal plans on either a dry erase board, blackboard, or projection screen. Be specific about what you want to accomplish during that rehearsal. Listing warm-ups, composer names, rehearsal markers, and measure numbers, along with the concepts to be addressed let students know the directed, musical mission for the day and also serve to inform them if that mission was accomplished. In addition, posting the objectives reinforces the concepts and approaches to preparation to be taught during the rehearsal.

The Band/Orchestra/Choir Business

The United States is regarded the world over as the leader in music pedagogy. Notice that word: *pedagogy*. Simply stated: American universities know how to teach people to teach music. Period. A degree from an American institution can carry quite a bit of credibility in other parts of the world because it implies that its recipient has truly been a part of the cutting edge of music education. Now, at the risk of angering some of my terrific colleagues, I would like to make some observations regarding this stature, because while I think that we do indeed set standards in teaching music education, we may sometimes miss the forest for the trees, or, perhaps, the soul for the brain.

The United States is one of the few places in the world that segments students early on with regard to the study of music. While general music certainly serves as a commonality among students, many of us later had to choose between, say, choir, band, or orchestra (note that these are large ensembles). With specific regard to the instrumental ensembles, almost all students began in a group setting, as opposed to private instruction. These young musicians then generally matriculate through the large group setting, possibly picking up private lessons along the way, and some even progress further onto a collegiate music experience. Some decide to major in music so that they can then recycle the process again for others or pursue a career in music outside of education. Sound familiar? The same the world over? Absolutely not. You see, the U.S. is one of the few places in the world that actually deems the large ensemble music experience important enough to not only be included in the school day, but actually is encouraged by its governing body (U.S. Congress) to do so. (Remember "No Child Left Behind.")

The vast majority of countries offer a more traditional (?) approach whereby young instrumentalists in particular study *privately*, sometimes for years, before becoming a part of a larger ensemble. Their music training will still include a large amount of general music and study of classic or multicultural styles, as well as performance as part of a choir. Ensemble skills, then, are often developed later because of early attention to individual skills—in other words, directly opposite what is commonly done in the States. So what does this mean or even effect? Well, how about considering artistic diet and depth of the human experience, to name a couple of things?

Okay, look: We are what we consume, whether it is food, drink, movies, art, or music—*whatever*. I objectively submit that what our system of pedagogy has done, while certainly bringing music to the masses, has been to possibly taint the experience where the future of *teaching* is concerned. We generally believe that for those wishing to teach or perform music as a profession, an audition and a degree are what are needed, and all is good. Stated another way—and pardon me for oversimplifying what is really a very complex issue with many variables—one begins at one end of the educational maze and at the other end grabs a degree stating that they're credible, musically inclined, and thereby worthy of their chosen path. Bing, bang, boom.

But there is one big problem with this.

While we're good at teaching people to teach music, we may not be consistent with teaching future educators to teach so that students will *learn*. We are terrific with the when's, why's, and especially the how's, but is that really teaching *music*? Or, are we focusing on the *business* of music? Not the music business, but the business of music. We can order busses, design marching shows, cultivate a booster program, get kids to show up at 6:30 a.m. (well, maybe 7:00 a.m.) and stay till the wee hours, make forms, create rubrics, standards, expectations, curriculums, schedules, programs, concerts, and on and on and on and on. But, what does any of that really have to do with *making music*? Sure, it has to do with readying the process, but what about truly imparting something to someone's soul? What about feeding ours?

Because we do something reasonably well doesn't mean that it should be our vocation. This is especially difficult because most of us have been told all of our lives that we're good at something, that something is our special gift, regardless of the size of our pond and its relevance to the size of our fish-self. Is, in fact, the true essence of what we do—being a musician first and foremost—getting lost under the guise of how organized, creative, forward-thinking, and detailed we are?

Here are two simple questions to ask yourself that might indicate where you are. First, how much time did you spend studying the score of one "serious" work that your ensemble performed last year (or a major work that you hope to someday perform)? Second, how does that time compare to the time you spent planning, say, a fall marching show or a choir festival? Or maintaining your feeder system? Or creating your weekly lesson plan? Or organizing your music library? Okay, okay—you get the point. Vince Lombardi once said, "Football doesn't develop character; it exposes it." Well, for those of us who stand in front of an ensemble on a regular basis, I would submit that conducting doesn't build musicianship. It exposes it. All the time spent off the box organizing our program will not improve nor affect that.

So I ask: Where are you? Are you spending time on the business or the art of music? And ultimately, what messages are you sending to the next generation about what music really is?

SIGNPOSTS

What:

Evaluating the business of music.

When:

Right. Now.

How:

Self-evaluation.
- Take a piece of paper and write "To Do" at the top.
- Write down everything that you're working on right now as well as things that need to be done.
- Go back through that list and put a check beside every item that does not literally pertain to making music.

Things like "tighten stands" do not count as pertaining to making music.

- What is left? And of that, how much time is spent on it?
- Ask yourself the question: business or art?
- Do this again periodically (say every few months/semester) to see if your focus is where you would like it to be.

WHAT GOES IN . . .

Let's talk food groups. While most of us can get close to naming all the basic food groups, many of us like to provide our own substitutions or additions to those groups. Chocolate, for example, should be its own food group. Anything grilled is in a subset of its own. Ice cream . . . well, you know. Of course, let's not forget recreational beverages. Or wine. And on and on. Of course, the trouble with many of these "food groups" is that although they are terrific for the moment and easily accessible, many don't make us "big and strong," as we tell our kids, but just "big." Moderation is one thing, but a steady diet . . .

In addition, the extended health risks are complicated. But, let's not forget what research has generally shown us, too. Our diet—and health—is often directly related to both our family and our friends. Yes, genetics plays a part, but I'm referring to the fact that we often eat or adopt the eating habits of those around us. In fact, what we eat sends a message about ourselves. And what we eat can have a profound effect on those around us. If I eat ice cream in the morning, I'm essentially saying to my kids that it's okay for them to do it. If I do it every morning, I'm saying that it's a normal breakfast. I know that seems a little ridiculous, but there is truth in that.

Now, let's look at them little folks. They grow up believing that ice cream is breakfast. As a result, as they go through key growth stages, chances are their bodies will not get the proper vitamins and nutrients needed. This can cause any variety of health problems, which could also lead to both intrinsic and extrinsic areas of psychological concern and mental health problems (kids can be innocently and honestly cruel when it comes to who they play with and why). What we eat, then, cannot only affect us, but also those around us and even those in our charge. And it begins with what we choose to put into our physical system. Make sense? Good. 'Cause now we're going to look at repertoire in that same context.

Again and again we've heard that repertoire selection is the most important thing that we do for our ensembles. I would, however, like to offer that our own repertoire consumption is equally as important, as I believe it has direct bearing on repertoire selection. What we're talking about here is the difference between hamburger and steak. Although there are a large variety and many incredible burgers out there, if we constantly eat hamburgers it can be difficult to fully appreciate great Texas, Kansas, Alberta, or Kobe beef. As a kid, I was hamburger crazy, and the first time I tried steak, I couldn't stand it. Why? I was judging it by the wrong rules. I mean, you wouldn't go to a baseball game and expect it to be officiated using the rules of football. Conversely, you wouldn't—and shouldn't—expect a great steak to taste like hamburger (with all due respect to my vegetarian colleagues). Still not quite making sense? Okay, maybe one of my earliest musical lessons might help.

My sister was a member of the Columbia Record Club years ago. You could buy one record at regular price and then get, say, twenty albums for a penny apiece, or something like that. Vinyl—remember?

Anyway, she snuck a copy of Iron Butterfly's "In-A-Gadda-Da-Vida" into the house. Can you imagine that dang, hippy, drug-crazed music in our Kansas household? Of course, I had to find a way to listen to this forbidden fruit. And I did.

The seventeen-minute title track of that album included the first and longest drum solo ever recorded to date. It was just over three minutes. Over and over and over I listened to it. Around this time in grade school, my teacher brought in another album by a band named "Bay Toven." At least, I though it was a band, until she informed us that this was, in fact, one of the greatest composers that ever lived. She advised us that we should love this music because it was written by this famous guy—who was *dead*. No problem, I thought. I may only be in the single-digit years of my life, but I'm pretty happening because I sneak listening sessions with my cool, big sister's albums. And then my teacher played some song by this dead guy. Song #9 as I recall.

And I listened.

And I waited.

Listened.

Waited some more.

And I never heard it.

I never heard the drum solo. How could this guy be so great if there was no drum solo? Of course, looking back, I was listening with the wrong set of ears, expecting rock music and not really expecting what I *did* hear because I had never heard any classical music to this point, let alone Beethoven. But now I had! And it did open up a new world for me!

Exposure was key. Whether hamburgers, rock music, or fine wine, the key is first being exposed to something, then through further exposure developing an understanding of quality within any given area. But, remember: If you only experience hamburgers, you'll never know or appreciate steak. Good hamburgers are fine, but a steady diet of them, well . . .

What's in your musical cupboard? What are you "eating?" What are you feeding your students? What type of musical health are you providing for them to pass on to those that they later encounter? We are what we consume!

SIGNPOSTS

What:

Repertoire—developing taste.

When:

Right now.

How:

1. Begin by jotting down twenty-five of your favorite pieces from your specific area: band or orchestra or choir.
2. Write down the twenty-five pieces you regard as most important to your genre.
3. Write down the names of five major American composers.
4. Write down the names of five prominent visual artists.
5. Write down the names of five living, best-selling authors of any genre.

6.   Answer the following questions. When was the last time I:

- attended a live concert of classical oriented music?

- attended any concert?

- performed on my instrument, whether as a soloist or with an ensemble?

- attended a play or musical?

- saw a movie?

- read a book?

- had an extended, not music-related conversation with someone?

Now, take a look at the answers you've provided. This should give you just a snapshot of a bit of what you're consuming and what influences not only your musical health, but also those you are in contact with. Keep in mind that it is *you* who must determine whether the results indicate healthy musical habits or not, as well as soulful growth.

Snapped Bolts

I've got an old Isuzu Trooper. It's the only car/truck I've ever purchased brand new, and it predates my wife (not her age, but our marriage). As a result, you can guess I have pretty strong feelings for "Suzy." She's got about two hundred-fifty thousand miles on her and has quite a history. Carried a lot of people, too. Conductors, composers, solo artists. I remember one time I had Maynard Ferguson and his Big Bop Nouveau crew to my high school. I thought it would be fun because I went to school with a few guys in the band and, hey, it was Maynard. He and the band showed up for rehearsal, blew through the combined BBN/high school band pieces, then attempted to chat with my students, who were still pretty much awed beyond the reasonable ability to think, let alone converse.

Although I said that the band showed up for rehearsal, I didn't say how they got to the rehearsal: They took the bus. I picked up Maestro Ferguson in the Trooper, which although much "younger" then, was obviously developing some real "character." As I drove MF to the rehearsal, we talked less about the schedule for the day and more about the history of the Trooper. He was obviously lovestruck with my girl. After the rehearsal, the entire band, with Mr. Ferguson in tow, headed back to the hotel for some down time before the evening concert. When the phone rang later, I was shocked that MF was calling ME. That's right: me. I had given my phone number to his manager, as any host would, in case there were any questions or needs. Well, evidently a need was so strong that Maynard called me to ask if I would pick him up for the gig—in the Trooper. Who was I to say "no?" It wasn't often I met someone who could recognize and appreciate the absolute highest level of automotive craftsmanship as well as the gentle ride offered by the Trooper.

Point is, there's some real history with Suzy and some pretty strong personal feelings as well. That's why I was so upset when one day, the hitch receiver finally tore away from the mainframe. No big deal, I reasoned. I would just take off the bumper and find someone to do some creative welding. To make diagnosis easier, I decided to go ahead and take the bumper off ahead of time to save time and money. That's when it happened. Of the eight bolts holding the bumper on, I snapped six off. Not stripped them, mind you, but snapped them in half. If you've never snapped a bolt before, let me tell you, it ain't a lot of fun. You have three choices depending what you're working on:

1. Drill the remaining bolt piece out, which can be a tedious process.

2. Have the other piece welded back on permanently (if it's big enough).

3. Throw it away.

My state frowns on vehicles running around without bumpers, so the third choice was not even an option. As it turns out, I was able to find a weld-wizard who made everything right with the world for me. Hitch, bumper, Suzy—all good. But, it got me thinking again. It got me thinking about burnout.

As conductors, how often do we cross the line from creating art to dictating and drilling? The relentless push for "perfection" that is realized in a spectacular rating or ranking? We've all heard of student burnout and I can attest at the collegiate level the number of students who are a part of music programs in high school who choose not to continue in college. I've spoken to many terrific students and the answer I hear most often is: "I need a break," which is the politically correct way of saying, "I'm burned out and am not finding a whole lot of intrinsic satisfaction out of the whole thing." Studies have proven that many students in high school don't take the class; they take "us." And no matter how much we love them and profess to care first and foremost for their musical wellbeing, how often have we pushed them too far and for what cost? Or maybe our balance is good professionally, but what about our own family? Stories abound in our profession about divorces, sons and daughters we never really took the time to know, or sordid student relationships. We push and push and push until something snaps, no matter how much we profess to love and care for it.

Egos do abound in the music business, which isn't a bad thing. The key is whether we use our ego in a healthy way or not. In my opinion, pushing only for perfection in the rehearsal room is not a healthy use of ego. Supporting possibility is. Please understand that I'm not saying that we sacrifice knowledge and expectation of subject matter, but I am saying that we must be vigilant that we don't "snap the bolts" by forcing both our professional and personal relationships to go where they don't want to—at least yet. As our profession seeks competition more and more as a means of musical justification, we're seeing more and more potential life-musicians and arts supporters bail out. That is not to say that competition as a tool is not good, but it is supposed to be a means to an end, not the end. But it's not only competition.

What we do every day in the rehearsal hall, studio, or classroom sends every bit as strong a message. Knowing when to torque and when to back off are essential. Truth is, I have snapped off many more bolts than just Suzy's. I have pushed students to false accomplishment, only to see them give up music after high school or even junior high. I did the very thing that I got into this profession not to do. In short, I had become what I despised. I could have done so much better if I had done two key things: watched and listened more. That's not easy. As conductors in a teaching situation, we walk a delicate balance between creating a nurturing, musical environment, and one in which there is the stereotypical teaching environment. How many times do we use our "teacher voice" when talking with students? Is it possible that our simple method of delivery could be confused with a science class, and is that good or bad? Of course, there's always a certain amount of "teacherness" that must take place, but couldn't a large part of creating a truly musically conducive environment actually be created off the podium, too?

There's a popular quote that I always try to remember: "People don't care how much you know until they know how much you care." It's been attributed to several people, but it's the wisdom it conveys that is most important. Both the creation and conveyance of art is based on relationships. Those relationships can be brush to canvas, pencil to paper, finger to keyboard, creator to performer, or ensemble to audience. How we foster and cultivate those relationships is not only crucial to the success of any given endeavor, but to the ability of any one person's willingness to express him or herself and support the expression of others through a lifetime.

One final thought: If it looks like you might snap a bolt, it's always good to get some help or advice from someone before it's too late. There are plenty of experienced welders out there. Chances are you even received your degree from a great one.

SIGNPOSTS

What:

Cultivating intrinsic and an artistic environment based on honest and sincere relationships.

When:

Any time, but best at the beginning of a semester or school year.

How:

1. Begin by observing without expectation. This is really one of the most challenging aspects of this process. How do students walk into the room? What is happening in other areas of their lives? Is it mid-term time? Are students over-extended? What are students talking to each other about before and after rehearsals or school?

2. Create a group of confidants. These might include other faculty, an administrator, a parent or two, students, other friends in the profession, or family. Inquire how these

individuals feel things are going with the program—be careful not to imply that there are any problems, except with faculty or mentors you trust. You must remain in control of the educational mission, but it is fine to show a willingness to both listen to opinions and incorporate great suggestions. A side note: It is amazing the perspective that your close friends and family will have of you. Don't be surprised if they offer an immediate, clear opinion. Besides, Einstein once said, "No problem can be solved from the same consciousness that created it."

3. Our best teaching often occurs in the hallway. Remember that quote from the reading? "People don't care how much you know until they know how much you care." By making contact with our musicians out of the context of the rehearsal room, we are able to have a bit more personal context in which to show that we do, indeed, care about *them*. While most student information is provided online at schools, there is additional information that I would encourage you to obtain, so long as it doesn't conflict with school policy or privacy. Here's what you do (note: this exercise works best at the beginning of a semester):

  • Get 3" x 5" note cards.

  • Put one student's name at the top of each card.

  • Put the card on students' assigned chairs.

  • On the board/overhead/PowerPoint, provide the following instructions: "Please provide the following information on your card. Be sure to put the question number down, but do not rewrite the question!" You can then decide what information you would like that is not already found in the school's student information. Examples include:

- Do you have other family members? Ages?
- Do you work? Where?
- What pets do you have? Names?
- What is your favorite kind of music?
- Who are your favorite artists or groups?
- What do you want to do after high school?
- What's the most exciting thing you've ever done?
- What is one of the things you dream of doing?
- Or whatever you can think of! (These cards also work for asking random questions in class. Just shuffle and see whose name comes up.)

Now, armed with this information you can stop a student in the hallway to compliment them on a part done well in rehearsal and perhaps suggest something for additional consideration next time, or inquire about something from their card. The idea is to foster a relationship and trust that extends beyond the teacher's needs, but incorporates that student's as well.

4. Have a H.A.T. conference with each student. H. A. T. stands for "How Are Things?" These can be formal or informal. During these chats you can open a dialogue about your program, other student academic concerns or successes, information from the student's card, whatever—the key is personal, one-on-one dialogue. How about suggesting a recording or private instructor? Now is the time.

Stick Monkey

I'm in a high school rehearsal, earlier in my career. It was the era when I was going to be the next greatest conductor in the history of the world, but nobody knew it yet, except me. It was the beginning of the year and students smart enough to take band would have the opportunity to be in my presence. As I was grandly waving through something (possibly Chance's *Variations on a Korean Folk Song*), I overheard a new student in the second row say to the person next to him, "I have no idea where we are. What should I do?" The student next to him replied, "Dude. Just watch the stick monkey." The *stick monkey*, not the "conductor" or better, "The Maestro!" It certainly gave me pause, to say the least (note the sly, Darwinian "paws" reference, thank you). What *do* we do up there? And how is it perceived?

Conducting. My old *Heritage of America* dictionary defines the root word as the following:

Conduct: (transitive verb)

1. To direct the course of; manage; control.
2. To lead or guide.
3. To lead an orchestra or other musical group.

4.　To serve as a medium or channel for conveying; transmit.

5.　To behave.

Hmmmm. Quite interesting and we're not even getting into defining "conducting" and "conductor." Students frequently have another view of what conducting is, one that may coincide with their parent's view: beating time. You know, the one thing that we learned in conducting class we're *not* supposed to do. 'Course, student's often call'em as they see'um.

Conducting. Conductor. I remember going through customs once, coming back into the States after some stick waving in Canada. The customs official asked me why I was in Canada. I proudly responded, so that he could later say he met me once, "I'm a conductor!" To which he questioned, "What railway?" In order to educate him, I grasped the teachable moment and said, "Not a railway. This kind of conductor," where upon I took to gesturing large, beautiful, artistic interpretations of nothing, carving the air into rainbows to shower down upon this poor, uncultured person.

He remained unimpressed.

I was then taken directly to security where I was rigorously questioned and my entire luggage recalled and searched for drugs—the only logical explanation for my behavior. Lesson learned there.

The *Harvard Dictionary of Music* provides a two-page explanation on both what conducting is and a brief history. There are a myriad of books and videos that seek not only to do the same, but also to improve upon what we do as conductors. For me, all the previous definitions provide the most accurate description of what we do—with emphasis on definition #4—despite the fact the many folks in our ensembles may think conducting is beating trace patterns and showing tempo.

I would suggest that the import is not defining what conducting is necessarily, but learning how to do it. That is to say, how can we accomplish the task at hand: conveying composer intent as filtered through a living, changing, organic performing medium with a myriad of variables, and beginning with the stick monkey up front? How about we start with the basics.

Allen's 12 Basic Tenets for Conducting

1. Know the score.
2. Know the score better. Contemplation serves to enlighten.
3. Have a definite process for score study and *use it*. (It's okay if it changes over time.)
4. Constantly ask yourself, "Why?" Why that title? That dedication? That note? That instrument? That dynamic? That phrase shape? That motive?
5. Conducting is our best and most efficient rehearsal tool.
6. The score dictates the appropriate gesture, not your ego or what feels good.
7. Showing is quicker than saying and can convey deeper meaning.
8. The conductor gives the tempo. It is the ensemble's responsibility to keep it.
9. Make the ensemble accountable for their music making.
10. No one is born a great conductor.
11. Watch rehearsals—with score if possible—of other conductors.
12. Constantly seek help or advice. Music in general—and conducting in particular—is learned best through mentorship.

While this list could go on, I have found these to be the introductory things to keep in mind regarding our craft. Number 10 needs particular emphasis. We've all been through those conducting courses where initially we're crammed full of the physical basics, because we need to learn the tools at our disposal. If we're lucky and the sequence is long enough, we not only learn a basic approach to score study, but we're also able to begin to combine these skills together. Notice the word "skills," rather than attributes. A skill can be developed; an attribute or disposition can't. Conductors get better because of deliberate, applied practice. They focus on elements of their ability to both glean information from the score and convey it to an ensemble. Fine *physical* conductors then, are made, not born.

That said, there is one extremely important reminder I need to make regarding being a conductor. You might recall this from another chapter: Conducting doesn't build musicianship; it exposes it. If one is a weak musician to start with, no matter how beautiful he or she looks, there will be nothing to "say." All the study and practice in the world will not suffice in place of a musical soul. The best artist educators are able to help students discover this soul and it is this soulful attribute that is basic to developing skills. A musical soul cannot be learned or created. It can only be exposed or strengthened.

There are so many terrific approaches to both the teaching of conducting as well as score study available now that everyone should be able to strengthen both their analytical and physical skills. However, the addition of a mentor and the ability to observe fine conductors in rehearsal is crucial to development. And, bottom line: We learn by doing. All the reading and thinking in the world will not get the job done. I used to fight in tae-kwon-do tournaments and I discovered a very simple truth: If you're going to be in a fight, you're going to get hit. Really. You will. Same thing with conducting. If you stand in front of an ensemble, you will always be a work in progress, if for no other reason than every piece brings with it new challenges.

But here's something to keep in perspective, which might help. Chances are, when you were taking conducting classes or at a symposium you were thinking, "Geez. I hope I don't look stupid." Or perhaps, "Geez, I hope they don't think I'm an idiot." Sound familiar? Now think about how you react when you're sitting in the ensemble, watching someone else. I'll bet you're not thinking those things about the person up front. I'll bet you're thinking, "Show me what you want." In fact, when we have those self-deprecating thoughts, we're being a bit selfish. Perhaps, instead of thinking about ourselves, we should be thinking about what the composer wants and how to convey it better. After all, it is his or her piece. But how can we begin that process right now? How do we move from being a living, breathing metronome to really being able to convey what it is we have gleaned from the score? And how can we make our musicians accountable for their music making as well? It begins with not just wanting to make music, but being *vulnerable* enough to follow through on that wish. Only then can any of us become more than a stick monkey!

SIGNPOSTS

What:

Re-establish or enhance a more musical communication through gesture. It is understood that these skills are primarily physical in nature and are presented in the spirit of their adaptability to support appropriate, gestural needs gleaned through rigorous score study. They are not an end unto themselves, simply a beginning as well as a review.

When:

Immediately

How:

Let's remember that the physical aspects of conducting are ground in simple human nature. We see something and we react. We've all heard the examples of how traffic cops are great conductors, but the real genius in what they do relies on their ability to use movements that are recognizable by anyone and don't have to be taught. While each traffic conductor has a very personal, unique style, it does not interfere with the clarity of what they are trying to convey and the ability of you or me to understand it.

Aside from viewing conducting as something that fosters a natural response, we must also remember that the majority of effective information comes from the face—especially the eyes. How do we know this? I could cite all kinds of research, but nothing proves it better than the last time you had a conversation with someone in person. Was that person sincere? Sad? Honest? Lying? In love with you? Happy? And how did you know? Simple: You inferred it from what you saw, in addition to what and how something was said. If we want to have a person's attention, if we want to tell them something important, if we want to know if they understand, we look at them. The same holds true when we're on the box. Conducting is what, when, and how. Too often, we focus on the "when" and not near enough on the "what" and minimal attention to "how." Do you like it when someone is talking and not looking at you? Might be something to ponder when we're conducting our groups ...

So let's get to it.

Posture

Let's begin with a review of the conducting stance. I want to preface this review—and all physical conducting commentary from here forward—with the idea that we, as conductors, want to work from a neutral, relaxed posture. Note the word "neutral." Our posture should enable us to immediately establish what we want to convey, rather than conveying something by itself, i.e. a tight baton grip indicates power, tension, hardness, volume, etc. To that end, I would suggest:

- A straight posture, imagining a straight line that encompasses the ankle, knee, hip, and shoulder. Be careful not to allow the head to drop. The head should be up, opening up the face to the ensemble. Adjustment can be made from there. An easy way to check your posture is to stand against a wall. Are your shoulders pulling away? Hips? Establish that posture line as best you can, but be sure to stay relaxed. There are a variety of exercises in many texts that can help you here, but the key is to retain what it feels like to be relaxed.

- I prefer a basic arm position that puts the forearms parallel to the ground, opening a larger, three-dimensional conducting space. Elbows should be comfortably extended just beyond the sternum. (Imagine placing a thin piece of board or pipe against your sternum. The elbows should be just forward of that "line.") In addition, the elbow position can be thought of as being at eight o'clock and four o'clock, but careful of not being too low, causing a disconnect between the face and the gesture. I often encourage my students, once they have established this stance, to:

  - Throw arms forward and relax into this stance, and

  - Think of C3PO from *Stars Wars* fame and how "properly" placed his elbows always were.

Baton Grip

There are a myriad of ways to hold the baton, especially as one looks at conductors from around the world. The idea behind grip is expediency—in other words, a grip that allows us to show more and talk less! The bottom line for me is a neutral comfort. I once imagined the baton as a direct extension of the arm. This led to an inflexible wrist and what was a mildly awkward position, greatly affecting horizontal motion. Remember that the main function of the wrist is in an up/down motion, with a sparing side/side motion. I do know conductors who have developed carpal tunnel syndrome over the years as a result of how they hold the baton. I tend to grip the baton as though shaking hands, with the knuckle nearest the fingertip of my right hand and thumb making first contact at the ferule of the baton. The rest of my fingers gently grip the baton, with the "bulb" being wrapped by my middle finger. My wrist stays in natural alignment with my arm, allowing the baton (with a correctly sized handle) to naturally extend at about a forty-five degree angle from my right hand. It is important that the wrist not extend up or down. Neutral position is the key. The angle created by this natural, relaxed position also puts the baton tip in the line of sight between conductor and ensemble, where adjustments can then be made based on the needs of the music. Remember: We meet our ensemble at the tip of the baton.

- Hinges: Know the hinges at your disposal, from smallest to largest:
  - knuckles
  - wrist
  - elbow
  - shoulder
  - chest

If the chest hinge is a bit mystifying, let alone its effect on music, think how you read the body language of those in your ensemble. How about that student that's slumping? You know, the one who looks like this rehearsal is the most painful thing in world. That's a great example of a closed chest hinge. Ever try to appear really, really happy while slumping? Or hug someone without extending your arms? Those are all examples of the importance of the chest hinge. Styles and the effect of music can be directly related to how we use all of those hinges. In general, the stronger and more rhythmic a piece, the more we may use our larger hinges, i.e. the elbow and shoulder hinges. The lighter the music, the more we may want to use our smaller, lighter hinges, like the knuckles or simply the wrist. The more legato/horizontal the music, the more we'll want to use a combination of the knuckle, wrist, and elbow hinges, maybe even adding a bit of shoulder.

Want to show JOY? Open up that chest hinge and be vulnerable! Want your ensemble to take a big breath? Open up that chest hinge and *breathe*! Hinges are one of the main keys to conveying style as well as one of the biggest problems for conductors. This is one of the areas where often times our conducting breaks down and we have to resort to verbal explanation. And remember, where words fail . . .

Ensemble sensitization:

Remember how I mentioned that different traffic cops have different styles? One of the best ways to begin to sensitize an ensemble is with the very first sound. Not yours. Theirs. Try the following sequence:

1. Pick a tempo and begin in 4/4. Have the students count each beat, beginning with "one" on each downbeat.

2. Add measures in 3, then 2. Perhaps 6, then 5. I even end in 13, 17, or 20.

3. Now, begin again on 4/4 and this time vary the tempo and add style, i.e. legato, staccato, marcato, etc.

4.   Do the above, changing the meter, too.

Other things to try include:

- Have students "sizzle" eighth notes and work odd meters and accompanying patters, like showing 5/8 as 2 + 3 (a 2-pattern), or 7/8 as 3 + 2 + 2 (in a 3-pattern).

- Have students play a scale in the key and meter of your choice and encompass varying style and tempi, as well as fermatas and caesuras.

By doing the above, you will find that the ensemble will have accomplished several things:

- They understand the value of looking up.

- They recognize your patterns.

- They recognize your affective gestures.

- They are comfortable looking at you for information, and

- You are comfortable looking at them, too!

One of the best uses of this approach is that you can incorporate all tempi, dynamics, meter changes, and phrase endings into a simple warm-up with deliberate practice, rather than having to take the time out of making *music* to explain or show a gesture! Do realize that the ensemble now expects to see what you want. Otherwise this just turned into a cool drill with no bearing on truly making music!

Now that we've done some introductory exercises, let's look at some ways that we can daily reinforce this visual synergy with our ensembles at the beginning of each rehearsal.

- Begin without a warm-up book. Start with only you!

- Use the Remington warm-up (descending chromatic scale starting on concert F and returning to that F between each pitch) or a scale of your choice. Inform the ensemble to sustain all sounds until you progress to the next scale degree on "my gesture." *Do not start with chords*. Part of the concept of this warm-up is to get both eyes and ears working!

- Use a good, clear gesture to begin the first sound—perhaps even just take a breath with the ensemble (without making an inhaling sound.)

- Change each pitch with as small a gesture as you can. Students will need to focus, but you can do it. Reinforce your belief in their ability to see the change and respond positively when they do! Be sure that the ensemble is matching pitch across the group as well as maintaining proper pyramid sonority.

- Incorporate stronger/softer style gestures as well as crescendos, decrescendos, fermatas—in short, all those things you worked on in the initial, gestural introduction above. Again, make sure that the musicians are also cognizant of sonority and pitch.

Additional techniques that encourage both watching and listening include:

- Use of the Curwin/Kodaly hand signs. Lots of creative and extremely useful possibilities.

- Fingers. Divide the ensemble into soprano, alto, tenor, and bass voices, assigning each group a number. Have all groups begin on the same pitch. Instruct the ensemble that when they see their group's number, they are to progress to the next scale degree. This will also require the ensemble to match pitch and adjust balance as they progress up and down the scale. You do not have to finish the scale!

- Occasionally slump, overconduct, or gesture from one side of your body to the complete other side. This is merely to keep the ensemble "honest" and to encourage response to a visual stimulus. Do not use this particular technique in the rehearsal proper!

- Conduct through a scale using only facial expression—no hands, arms allowed.

- As mentioned in an earlier chapter, "monk," silent, or "stealth" rehearsal sequences (where you are not allowed to speak) are terrific for focus.

- Stop conducting time/tempo and only reinforce phrase, volume, or style. This could be the most challenging thing you do! Inform the ensemble that it is their responsibility to continue to play, even if you stop conducting—there is a difference between not conducting and stopping a group. The idea is to think in super-metric terms, to show direction and shape across the bar lines. Trust the ensemble and be ready for them to trust you.

Knowledge Is Not Wisdom

I started driving when I was very young. Mostly tricycles at first. From there I moved on to bicycles and then to a mini-bike. Oh, the wind through my hair at eighteen mph. About that time I also learned to drive a tractor, a part of growing up in the Midwest with parents from rural backgrounds. It is often a necessity on the farm to have children who can drive power equipment while someone "older" does the specific labor required. It was logical, then, to move from tractors to trucks several years before legal driving age. I don't mean driving on the road, but in the pastures and fields. From brush-hogging (a way of mowing using a tractor and a five- to six-foot mower pulled behind) to throwing hay to setting posts, driving was kind of important to get things done around home. When I was getting close to restricted license age, I had been behind the wheel for a few years. Still, I remember when my dad said, "Go drive the truck around in the pasture for practice." Wow. I had just won the lottery. I tore off and went into the back pasture in our old, white, Ford F100. I had started driver's education classes so I was getting "book-smarted" on driving, too. In fact, I had spent some time in recent weeks correcting my parents and grandparents on their driving skills, as well as quizzing them constantly. I had no idea how they had not been a part of a major accident every day, because it was clear they did *not* understand the rules of the road. I, of course, did. Because I had read them. And passed quizzes on a regular basis. So, I'm headed into the back pasture at whatever speed my heart desired. I should add that this was before seatbelts were mandatory. This was to be my first memorable lesson in gaining wisdom. Nothing huge, but still very memorable.

I really put the coals to her out back. As I reached speeds upwards of a screaming thirty mph, I made sure that my hands were in the proper position, that I was checking for obstacles—like our horses—and I even calculated proper breaking distances. Everything was as it should be for the perfect, well-read driver. Then I hit the first of the terraced spots in the pasture. The closest I had to the kind of sensation I felt then was the first time I wrecked on my Schwinn Orange Peeler, later followed by the Honda Mini-Trail wreck when I was going to fast jumping ditches and had to do a mid-air bailout.

Thankfully, in both those cases, the ground broke my fall, but not any bones. The truck went airborne just enough that when it landed, it bounced on one, then two more, and finally the fourth of the tires. The old Ford pitched, lurched, and danced as I was jostled sideways in the seat, my hands flying off the wheel and, luckily, my foot off the accelerator. I guess in looking back, jostled isn't the right word, since the truck landed so hard that I actually bounced up and hit my head on the cab roof before landing in the center of the bench seat. In that split second, as it was happening, I remembered being born, my first birthday, my favorite tricycle, my first-grade teacher Mrs. Ashby, beating up my Cub Scout pack, starting band, every day of junior high school, getting my Selmer Mark VI alto saxophone, my first kiss (thought I was a worm being swallowed by a big-mouth bass), and even more memories: basically that avalanche of recollections the brain pushes through you just in case whatever stupid thing you've just done doesn't work out so well.

As the truck rolled to a stop, I realized that I might survive. When I looked around and didn't see my dad, I was sure I was going to survive. The truck was undamaged, but I still wasn't aware just what had happened to me, the perfect driver. My hands had been in position, I was sitting up straight, I was at a manageable speed, and the horses were all in the other pasture. My knowledge had served me well. But at that point, I realized that wisdom had suddenly found its way into my driving education: I learned that when you're driving, anything could happen at any time. My speed was clearly too fast for the terrain, a seatbelt might have been a good idea, and it's amazing that a motor vehicle can hit the ground so hard that your hands can come off their required clock-face positions on the steering wheel if you're not gripping tightly. All the reading and studying in the world didn't quite prepare me for actually having the kind of freedom I was allowed and I was too confident to know better.

Strangely enough, I'll bet many of us have had that same type of experience, but in a different setting. Remember when you first took conducting? Or your first student teaching experience? Or your first position as a full-time music educator or performer? Conducting class was more like driver's education than anything else I've experienced. We all learned the textbook way of doing things, including hand positions, conducting patterns, styles, gestures, winks, nods, etc. In fact, we learned them so well that we realized very quickly all of the things our band or orchestral conductors were doing wrong. Heck, we even wondered how some professionals ever got jobs based on what we were seeing. Man, were we ever needed in our profession! Soon, however, we stood in front and, oh my, was there a change in perspective. We had the knowledge, for sure, but the wisdom was lacking. Student teaching and our first jobs followed suit, didn't they?

We have come to believe what we see, what we read, and what we're told. It's safer and much easier that way. Even our score study pursues the definitive interpretation, often times taken from someone else's approach. The definitive recording, performance, statement, or insight are all in the mix, too. But, at best, all these things only provide knowledge. They only add to what we know about something. The value of wisdom is also becoming a more and more difficult thing to acquire in this day and age because of a society that values expediency. Expediency is the archenemy of wisdom. What we must do is take the time to think, concentrate, meditate, and/or ponder. It is the action of inaction that allows us to take knowledge and experiences and polish them into pearls of wisdom. The only definitive performance is our own, because there is no one else in the world with the same experiences and knowledge each one of us carries within.

I lived for a time on the Cheyenne River Sioux Reservation in South Dakota. One of the most important skills that I have tried to retain from that experience is the ability to let some things work themselves through in their own time. You may have heard of the phrase, "doing things on Indian time." Some people regard this as meaning, "It'll get done when it gets done." They couldn't be more wrong. It means that the time isn't necessarily quite right, that something will happen when it is ready. This ability to be patient, to think, to listen to oneself and others, and to trust oneself is, for me, at the core of what develops wisdom. Silence is really anything but! It is a way of clearing the way for the subconscious to be heard. The wisdom of the composer lies before us, but are we diligent enough, and then patient enough, to glean it? What about our ensembles? Are we truly both hearing and "seeing" them? Or do we continue to turn the ears off, only to be able to continue to dispense the "definitive" information we have taken from someone or somewhere else, without contemplating it first? Wisdom, then, is not a destination, but a pathway—one in which we not only continue to tread, but one which can also allow our musicians to grow by means of our journey.

SIGNPOSTS

What:

Finding ways to begin the journey from knowledge to wisdom.

When:

This moment.

How:

1. Stop. Just stop. Put this book down in just a moment and think about why you've read this far. There's a reason this chapter appealed to you, if it did. Chances are, you're searching for something. Now it's time to stop and focus on what that something is. Perhaps you know it, or it may be knocking on your subconscious. Regardless, it's time to

give it its due. Turn off any music, TV, computer—whatever could distract you—and be alone with your thoughts. Focus on the one thought in particular. Don't expect to have the answers suddenly come to you. In fact, you may later choose to do something completely away from the subject matter at hand. Many times, as you know, the answers come to us when we least expect it. That's because we allow the subconscious to work on something that's not directly related to our current task.

2. Try doing something completely unrelated to what you're focusing on. Go to a movie, walk the dog, build a house. Then, come back with a fresh, revitalized mind. Amazing what a fresh perspective can do.

3. Put the score down. Walk away. Go outdoors. Breathe. It starts there.

4. Have a chat with a friend. Ask how he/she is doing. Be human. Perhaps they might have a perspective on something you've been working on. Be open to any suggestions or insights. Hearing someone else ponder your situation can sometimes free you just enough to see the answer!

5. If you really listen to that inner voice, you will find that it is telling you right now what you need to do in order to "tap in." The challenge is being vulnerable and quiet enough to hear that voice and to trust it. Do it now. You may not know it, but you're waiting on yourself.

DEER EARS

A s you may have surmised, I spend a lot of time observing things, especially in the thick of nature whenever possible. Part of this, I'm sure, is my central Kansas upbringing. I was one of those kids that could come home from school and be down at the neighbor's pond within ten minutes. We always had horses as well as a big garden, some chickens and pigs on occasion, and lots of hay, straw, and feed. As a result, we also had abundant small wildlife. Mice, skunks, possums, raccoons, coyotes, and all manner of indigenous snakes were part of my childhood. I relished observing all these critters as well as listening to all the sounds around me, which were absolutely spectacular. I have, on occasion, taught some of these sounds to ensembles I have conducted by assigning specific groups both the animal sound and its accompanying rhythm, and then combining everyone together to teach part responsibility—and listening.

Even now I have a preoccupation with "natural sounds." Perhaps you do, too. Your car, for example: Do you find yourself picking up the tempo from the turn signal? Or the windshield wipers? What about the arrival pitch of an elevator, just before the doors open? Some elevators sound a pitch as they begin to move, although most signal arrival (so as to allow us to bring to closure any conversations we may be having and to ready ourselves to exit from our short, amusement park-like ride). One hotel elevator I found particularly interesting. It sounded a melodic major third when going up, but a melodic minor third when going down. I found this humorously depressing. It was as if going up was literally uplifting, carefree, motivating, inspiring, even heavenly! But, going down, was . . . going down. Anticlimactic, underachieving, losing, descending to the depths, perhaps just a stepping stone before descending into the inferno. Beeps, honks, squawks, smacks, slaps, yelps, bells, whistles, whirrs—music is all around us. But do we really hear it all? Do we really hear our own ensembles? And if so, are we listening?

You can learn a lot about both hearing and listening from an animal. I find it quite fascinating that the rabbit is born to listen, while the human to make sound. The most beautiful thing about watching any animal is that they live in that moment, so anything that is seen, heard, or felt triggers a primordial response to determine if it is a threat, meal, or mate. Amazing. Take a deer, for example. A deer, when startled, has a three-step process it will generally follow based on a "stimulus." First, it will freeze, trying not to be seen while trying to gain more information by sight, sound, and smell. Second, if needed, it will run for cover, then repeat the process. The third reaction is to completely bail out and run away as fast as possible, though at some point it will return to step 1.

What I find most interesting of all is how the deer actually hears. You see, a deer does not have "fixed" ears, that is to say, a deer's ears have independent motion. This is one of the reasons that deer can hear so well. They can actually turn one ear toward the direction of the sound. In addition, the size of a deer's ears serves to amplify sounds, sort of like a hairy satellite dish. Most interesting, however, is that despite numerous stories of how well deer can hear, the fact is that the hearing range for both deer and humans is very, very similar. The difference? Deer recognize immediately any sound not common to their environment (which is also why deer can become acclimated to various environments over time, like zoos). Again, they don't just hear; deer listen! Now, I realize at this point you must be thinking that I've truly spent too much time sitting in the woods watching deer. Well, maybe, but they still have stuff to teach me. One of the things they taught me is that they would be GREAT conductors, except they don't speak human and can't hold a baton in their hoofs. But I can, and that got me thinking again.

The finest musicians/conductors that I've observed or worked with generally have incredible ears. Not okay ears, but incredible ears. They've learned the value of not only hearing, but also listening, and they know what to listen for because they've spent time understanding the score or part and have very, very specific expectations derived from that study. Like a deer, they, too, can hear what doesn't belong or what might be a "musical threat." But are these people especially gifted? Do they have a special acuity that others do not? Or, have they simply learned to really listen, honed by experiences, which have set appropriate benchmarks for them? This points out one of the key characteristics of true artists: their perseverance in going after the sound they need to hear. What distinguishes the great from the good is that they never merely accept "good enough." The good play; the great *communicate*. And this, colleagues, begins with not just hearing, but listening. From there, we can use the techniques, suggestions, and discoveries at our disposal to get the sound we desire to hear.

But, to truly listen, there is one tremendous barrier that we must overcome: our eyes.

Sight can rob us of our ability to hear and truly listen. Need an example? Try this little experiment. Have a student in your ensemble read an article or a bit of a chapter out of a book, maybe even the program notes from a score. As the student is reading this (silently or out loud, which is my personal favorite because the other members of the ensemble can hear what's going on, too) tell them an anecdote or story, possibly something that happened to you that morning. Now, ask the student to summarize both what was just read and what you just told them. And be ready for them not to be able to do it. At best, they will have been able to focus on one thing. Why? Because they haven't developed the skill set to listen in this way yet and because humans aren't naturally hard-wired to do so.

Now before you say, "So what?" let me point out that this scenario is exactly what we demand of our students, as well as ourselves, in rehearsal every day. The members of our ensemble are looking at music and hearing a cacophony of sounds, just as we are up front. The ability to process this kind of information is not available to us. What we must do is to understand two things. First, reliance on the eyes can take away our ability to truly listen rather than simply hear, and, second, we need to be able to direct our listening. This could be toward an instrument, vocalist, section, or performance space, to name a few options.

Incidentally, this little exercise also points out the importance of being comfortable with what we're looking at so that we can throw off the ball and chain of visual dependence. We, and our ensembles, need to have ingested the music enough so that we are not bound to the print. This will open not only our ears, but also our eyes, allowing both conductor and ensemble to experience both listening and responding to gesture in new and invigorating ways! Remember: The rabbit, as well as the deer, was born to listen. And, I think, maybe we were too.

SIGNPOSTS

Developing the ability to not only hear, but to listen, for both our ensembles and us.

When

Immediately!

How

Here are a few exercises to try for both you and/or your students.

The sounds around us . . .

1. In just a moment, close this book and then your eyes. With your eyes closed, count how many sounds you can identify. These sounds can include conversations, birds, doors opening, anything. Go ahead—try it!

2. Do the same as the previous exercise, except this time try to focus on each individual sound. Focus on that conversation and feel as if you are sitting right there. Hear the running water and be present. The sound of the coffee pot finds you

standing right beside it. In other words, shift your hearing from one, clear sound event to another.

3.   Live in that world, or at least continue to develop the ability to do so whenever you can. Out with friends? Driving, walking, or biking somewhere? At the mall or the park? Hear first, and then direct your listening.

Deer Ears . . .

Remember that reinforcement is absolutely essential in the listening process. It's one thing to get our ensembles to "hear like a deer"; it's quite another to continue to expect and encourage them to!

1.   Explain how a deer "hears." If you want, use your hands as extended deer ears on top of your head, moving them as explained in the story.

2.   Explain to the ensemble that you are all now going to say your ABCs together at normal speaking volume while "cupping" your ears as if trying to hear something.

3.   Demonstrate that during the course of this little exercise, everyone can cup their ears in any direction, i.e., both hands behind the ears, in front, one behind and one in front, or completely covering the ears.

4.   Recite the ABCs!

5.   Ask your ensemble what they heard and to be specific. Sometimes it's so obvious that they don't realize what they heard. This is the bridge to listening! Could the low brass hear the percussion? Did the second row hear only the front row? How about only the third row?

Inside the sound . . .

Pick the scale of your choice. Designate your tuba (or lowest instrument) as the conductor, since they will lead the scale. The guidelines are simply:

1. The "conductor" cannot perform the scale in regular tempo and should play with a normal volume. In addition, it is better to move to the next note slower rather than faster to allow the ensemble to hear and listen.
2. The ensemble starts when they hear the tuba.
3. The ensemble changes notes when they hear the note change.
4. If you would like students to close their eyes, you can simply clap your hands twice when you want them to stop!
5. Now, designate a horn, flute, or trumpet as the conductor! This will direct the hearing toward a different timbre, as well as cause the balance of the group to adjust.

Listening out!

Either during a scale, chorale, or rehearsal proper, challenge students to hear:

- only themselves
- the person to their immediate left or right
- the person two or three people in either of the directions above
- the first person in the section (always for pitch, anyway)
- the last person in the section

Again, the idea is to create opportunities for direct listening—hearing like a deer. One of the first steps in the actual rehearsal process is to make sure that musicians understand their musical role in any composition. They shouldn't "MISS" anything. In other words, everyone should know if they are either:

- **M**elody
- **I**nner part (or countermelody)
- **S**upport **S**ystem (I'm not fond of what the word "background" implies.)

A simple show of hands or a directed question can solve a lot of problems and solidify an understanding of musical roles at any point in a composition.

These exercises, as well as a quick review of those found at the end of *Silent Conversations*, can now serve as the template for directed listening in rehearsal and performance. Now, listen with deer ears!

The Conductor in Rehearsal

My first lesson in conducting was on a Saturday morning, in the single-digit years of my life, from an internationally recognized superstar. I'll never forget the impact that this legend had on me and surely countless others. Even to this day I carry his image in my mind. Quite a powerful experience. I speak not of Bernstein, von Karajan, nor Carlos Kleiber, but of the one, the only: Bugs Bunny. The episode was entitled "Long-Haired Hare" and in it, Bugs assumed the identity of Leopold Stokowski in an effort to exact revenge on an opera singer.

What struck me was the way the characters reacted to Bugs as he appeared in "costume." I didn't know this "Leopold" who was being referred to in such revered tones, but it was obviously someone of great import. Then, the command of the vocalist and the ensemble from the podium! I was mesmerized by what I was seeing and truly intrigued as to who and what this character was. That experience began the journey I am still on today and will be on tomorrow. As an instructor of conducting at the university, camps, and symposiums, I find it quite interesting how much I still see that original image of Bugs. I don't mean that in a condescending or humorous way, but in the same way that I saw myself. Let me explain.

My first attempts at the physical, analytical, and psychological aspects of conducting probably occurred in junior high school, where I was allowed to wave through a piece during rehearsal. Of course, this dealt only with the "physical" and even then, only with beating time. But I still remember how I approached that experience: with the same demeanor that I had thought I had seen on every conductor up to that point. As a student conductor in high school and into the early part of my career, it was also similar. I figured if I knew how the music went and kept time, all was good. As long as I acted like those I had seen on a podium before, all would be fine. In other words, I was trying to be the stereotypical conductor, basing what I did on my perceptions of what conductors really do. I wanted to look and act like I thought conductors should look and act.

Part of my thought process then was based on the idea that there is a right way and a wrong way to do things—that chase for the "definitive" approach. As humans, it is only natural to rely on what is most comfortable to us in times of stress and it is sometimes helpful to assume the guise of someone else in just such a stressful situation. As teachers, musicians, conductors, and artists we don the shrouds of those before us. It is natural and fine to do so, but the challenge is to move past this assumed identity in order to discover our true, musical self. Our true podium presence, it must be remembered, is hugely influenced by what we do off the box.

Frequently I see young conductors concerned with the following:

- looking competent and not embarrassing themselves
- looking beautiful
- conducting the time signatures and, occasionally, some dynamics
- looking like they think a conductor should look

The paradox is that none of these have to do with making music, let alone finding our inner conductor. Perhaps this is the fault of instruction or at least the time constraints that many universities are under in the time allotted to teach conducting.

There is also a development of understanding that can be observed in conductors. That development is based on one crucial skill: score analysis. Or to be more precise: in-depth score analysis. Without this, there is nothing to "say." Liken it to doing a book report. If you don't read the book, there ain't gonna be a decent report. The report will simply turn into word-padding and incoherent drivel, even though there are references to the book. Likewise, without proper score analysis, an overall clear, concise view of a piece will not present itself, preventing the conductor from even beginning to portray composer intent.

Today, thankfully, there are a huge number of books on the market that address not only score analysis, but a variety of conducting issues. And, of course, there are absolutely incredible, living resources/mentors out there who can help anyone get better at what they do.

Let's not forget deliberate practice and work ethic, too. The ability to rehearse with purpose and perspective depends on those two things. Are you nervous when you get on the podium? Perhaps it's because you don't know the score well enough to have made those decisions that will propel the group forward. If you've been in a situation in which you had secured some wisdom from your score study and had a definite musical direction, I would wager that your rehearsal had specific focus and that the time seemed to fly by too quickly. If you walk in front of an ensemble and think to yourself, "Well, let's just start here and see what's up," chances are that rehearsal will either last forever or you will progress slowly. A good ensemble will eat you up if you're not prepared and, if not prepared, you will have no chance of serving as the composer's advocate.

Think it's easy to do a fine honor band, all-state band, or professional group? It may be enjoyable, but it's not easy. If you don't have the experience yourself, ask those who do. It's kind of like driving a Formula-1 car versus a Toyota Camry: The Formula-1 car may go faster and with more control, but if you don't take the time to learn to drive, neither speed nor control will do you a bit of good. Whether you're working with a top-notch professional ensemble or a middle school band, there's a lot to prepare for, and you still need a definite grasp of what you're going to do and whom you're working with. It is an absolute necessity that you understand the value of having something to musically say, as well as the ability to move the group musically forward in an economy of time.

Okay, so let's say we know the score, we're ready for rehearsal, we get in front, and we're off to the races. We have so much to say, explain, educate, and pontificate about that we can barely contain ourselves. Perhaps we don't contain ourselves and we relate every factoid, technique, explanation, and approach that we have devised. That's problematic, too. Problem is, research indicates that most people get better at doing stuff by actually doing stuff, not by just "hearing" about it. In other words, if an ensemble is going to get better at performing a piece, then usually it's a good idea to actually play the instrument and the piece. Less talking, more musical "walking."

I used to spend so much more time yapping. I would provide information and incredibly insightful detail into whatever I could. The composer, the piece, my life, your life, moments, events, jokes, tear-jerking stories, bursts of anger, and all manner of ways of trying to illuminate what I wanted in the piece at hand. I eventually realized that I was preventing the ensemble from actually playing (which is why most of us dove into music in the first place), and also that what I was saying was becoming increasingly meaningless because there was just too much of it. I noticed this when I began taping myself early in my career. Watch two minutes, throw up in a trashcan, get angry, think about pumping gas for a living, repeat the process.

I noticed something physically, too. At that time, I felt that I needed to give the grandest, largest, and most spoon-fed conducting gestures that I could, to enable the musicians to play. But by watching video of myself, I learned that, in contrast, I was getting in the way of the music by constantly trying to enable everything that happened. This issue, I feel, is one of transition. It is the transition from being a player within the ensemble to becoming the conductor in front of the ensemble. While the conductor should never stop thinking as a player and considering what a player needs, the conductor must also be both judicious and vulnerable in what be or she offers to the ensemble. Too much gesture is similar to too many words.

Perhaps even more important is that the musicians in the group need to be allowed to be accountable for their own playing. The best conducting in the world, as an example, will not fix poor counting by a player. We need to trust our musicians, expecting that they will bring something to the musical equation. We're talking less is more here—both in what we choose to portray or explain in an effort to move rehearsal forward.

And that's where our skills of observation and language come in.

When was the last time you watched a rehearsal by one of the leading conductors? There are a myriad of incredible rehearsal snippets online now, making conductors such as Gustavo Dudamel, Carlos Kleiber, David Robertson, and many of those no longer with us, available. Likewise, great DVDs are readily available, featuring artists like Frederick Fennell, H. Robert Reynolds, Craig Kirchhoff, Eugene Migliano Corporon, Jerry Junkin, Allan McMurray, Richard Floyd, and a host of others. At no other time in the history of conducting have so many resources been available.

Still, nothing beats actually being there and hearing, watching, and feeling the rehearsal "vibe" in the room. I remember once observing a two-hour rehearsal with Bob Reynolds as he worked with one of the regional military bands on some terrific literature. I vowed to write down everything he said. And I did. Two hours later I had only filled a half-sheet of notebook paper and the longest sentence he said contained seven words. In two hours. I went to find a trashcan to throw up in (again) and ponder pumping gas for a living.

At its best, our job as conductors can be defined as blatant musical enabling—enabling the musicians to make music themselves, without us. To enable in a musical environment means we must allow a degree of vulnerability, That means that when we're doing our job well, we're able to let our *musicians* perform while providing not only those bits of support as needed, but the overall architecture and trajectory of the musical work. Think about that for a moment. We should encourage and support our musicians so fully that we are not musical dictators, but rather partners in the musical recreation of a composer's captured moment of improvisation. We must allow our musicians to be at least an equal part—or more—in the process of music making.

Remember: *They're* the ones with the instruments. A baton doesn't make a sound. If we can allow our musicians their space, then we can actually put ourselves in a position where instead of acting as musical traffic cops or crime scene investigators, we can truly bring our musical experience, score wisdom, inference, and passion to the rehearsal room and concert hall—in part, the very same thing we expect of our ensembles! I don't think it makes a difference whether we stand in front of musicians in their second year or the most accomplished group. The only qualifier should be the amount of pedagogy required by the ensemble to accomplish a given musical task, but not at the sacrifice of the music itself.

So, what is our job in rehearsal if it's not to tell the musicians exactly what to do at all times? Not during a performance, mind you, but during the ensemble's period of musical incubation? There are many answers to that question, beginning with the kind of musicians we are, our skills, our life experience, the ensemble, the piece, the rehearsal environment, and so on. Perhaps, however, we can look at ourselves objectively and by analyzing what we do, discover what either works for us or ways that we can help foster a better musical synergy with the ensemble. At the very least, we can begin by letting our musicians bring their own skill, their own emotion, their own acquired musical knowledge to the piece, rather than imposing the conductor's vision on the music that they are making. It is then that we can begin to get the space between the notes to leap off the page

SIGNPOSTS

What

Suggestions for improving our rehearsal skills and enabling our ensembles to bring what they have to the musical equation.

When

Immediately.

How

There is no formal process to follow to reach this goal. Your own power of observation is of paramount importance here. You will need that video recording you made earlier. Of course, you can always make another, but use a rehearsal video, not a performance video.

1.   Watch the video, notating not just teaching techniques as you did in *Webs*, but also focusing on the nonverbal elements of your rehearsal.

2.   The questions below are designed to guide you through what you observed. Notice that there are no right/wrong statements. All questions are designed to have you make decisions based on your own observations and your own unique skills and attributes. While some conducting best practices are universal, what you should seek is a path of discovery and wisdom specific to you rather than a prescriptive list.

     •   How does the conductor enter the room? What message does his/her demeanor send?

     •   How does the individual appear on the podium? Does that person look like someone you would want to perform for?

     •   How is the conductor's posture? Open? Inviting?

     •   What does the conductor's face say? Can you see his or her face?

- Is there eye contact between the conductor and the ensemble, some kind of musical conversation?
- Does the conductor "cut off" or release?
- Does the conductor evoke sound or "attack?"
- Does the conductor's speech mirror the piece? In other words, is the speaking style in the affect of the piece (i.e., slow piece = relaxed, direct delivery)?
- Does the pulse seem to continue even when the ensemble ceases to play?
- Does the conductor acknowledge the players, especially after requesting something?
- Does the conductor always conduct?
- During how much of the rehearsal does the conductor speak? Twenty percent? Thirty percent? Fifty percent?
- How big are the gestures?
- Is there any information besides time signature?
- How much variation and musical reinforcement is there in the pattern?
- Does the conductor tend to lean into the personal space of the ensemble, almost willing them to make something happen?
- How does the conductor handle nonmusical issues?
- What is the general volume of the conductor's voice?
- Does the conductor only point out "mistakes" (reactive rehearsing) or is attention paid to what's good or improved (proactive rehearsing)?

FUEL IN THE TANK

Two things in this world drive me nuts: having to get fuel for a vehicle and tying sneakers. Of the two, getting fuel seems to be the most challenging for me. Running out of gas is almost a hobby. It's not because I'm lazy. No, it's something far deeper than that. It's a combination of the "how far" challenge as well as the "I don't have time" conundrum. You may recall Suzy the Isuzu Trooper. She had been my trusted "pony" for some twenty years. In that time, I've run her out of gas more times than I can remember. Every time resulted in both frustration and, if I was open to it, acknowledging the beauty of the moment. Or an intrusion by the police. Allow me to explain.

I was driving home very late at night from a gig with a nine-piece swing band that I used to perform with. Of course, I was low on gas getting to the gig, but heck, I could make it. I could maybe even make it home. As I was driving home after the gig, I began my incantation to the God of Fossil Fuel, just in case there really is one. Which I think there is. But he/she does have selective hearing. Anyway, the fuel light came on. When that happened, I knew that meant that I had about five to ten miles to take care of business.

As the miles passed behind me, my incantations turned into flat-out promises to both the God of Fossil Fuel and to myself. (C'mon, we've all vowed to "never get in this situation again.") The God was not listening this evening. The Trooper started to sputter. But I knew what to do. The fuel injector for Suzy is located in a spot in the fuel tank that is not the lowest point. I discovered early on that if I swerved from from side to side while driving, much like a giant slalom skier, I could swish the gas around in the tank enough that I might be able to make just a mile or two more—sometimes longer. So here I am, about 2:00 a.m., on a county highway in a rural area, swerving from side to side. On a weekend. And, sure enough, I see the lights flashing in the rear-view mirror. The GoFF had heard me, but decided to delegate tonight's request to the local gendarmes.

I pulled over, knowing that when I stopped swerving, I was abso-lutely sunk. I rolled the window down and waited, looking in my side mirror for the familiar walk. Now, my truck looked a bit, shall we say, *weathered*, so I completely understood why the officer began shining his flashlight into the back of the truck. After seeing fishing poles, a lawn chair, parts of an old gorilla costume, old tools, torn clothes, and trash bags, the officer moved his free right hand down to his sidearm and unsnapped the leather strap that keeps the weapon secure. He gen-tly gripped its handle. The first time I had seen this, I was nervous, but I'd had a bit of experience by then.

When he shined his flashlight directly in my face, I sensed that I wasn't quite the suspect he had pictured. I'm sure the tuxedo I was wearing helped. Before he asked me if I knew why he stopped me, he spied my gig bag in the back seat. He asked me what the bag was and I told him that it was an instrument and that I was coming home from a gig. Then, inevitably, he wanted to know if I knew why he stopped me. I said yes, because I'm an idiot. He then asked me if I had been drinking. I said no, but that I wish I had some alcohol to put in the fuel tank. He then put it all together and relaxed. He did ask how many miles I had on the truck. When I responded, he simply stated, "I think you got your money's worth." Then he asked what instrument was in the gig bag and, of course, whether I had ever heard of, or met, Kenny G. The officer's unsolicited musical opinions and brief musical history followed and for a moment in time, we shared a common bond through music.

I still find it incredible that when you mention anything about music, most people have some kind of response. Some apologize for not having "a musical bone" in their body. They actually apologize. Others relate their experiences singing or playing an instrument. Wow. And usually all this is unsolicited. What a unifying, powerful experience. Walk into a crowded room and announce you were on a state champion football team and some folks may say "nice work" before moving on to another conversation group. Mention that you're a musician, however, and you'll begin to hear stories about everyone else's music experiences as others walk up to your group. Interesting, though, how "others" are able to relate experience. They are generally able to qualify it as something they did before moving to something else.

We don't get off quite so easy. Let me give you an example: a window. When most people look out a window, they see a live picture framed by the window they are looking out of. They might see a lawn, trees, people walking, a blue sky, clouds, birds, a car driving by, and so on. But musicians—we look out a window and we are working. We're cataloguing what we see into an effective fuel supply to use later. We don't just see, do we? We actually process both consciously and sub-consciously what we feel when we look out that window and at some point we will relive that affect, often in a musical context. For instance:

- How a clear, blue sky makes us feel.
- The wind whispering "good morning" through corn stalks on a hot summer day.
- The shuffle-funk rhythm of the subway train approaching the station.
- The gentle breath on our cheek of a sleeping baby.

Yet, despite how we may view the world and what goes on in it, do we take the time to truly sense it? Do *you* take the time to truly sense what it feels like to live in this world?

We give so very much to this music vocation. Many of us feel that we must devote everything we have to it and to our students, and that if we don't, we're short-changing them. The reality, however, is that we're cheating ourselves. We are artists. We are musicians. The fuel for what we do is the life we choose to live, the life we take notice of. If we don't take the time to refuel ourselves, we will end up swaying side to side in front of those who have entrusted us. In time, we will run out of fuel and most likely in a deserted place. And that's when we'll most likely remember all of the refueling stations we passed but were too busy or too ambitious to stop at.

I remember watching the great conductor Simon Rattle in rehearsal with a collegiate group. After working a particular piece for some time, he suddenly stopped and asked the ensemble a question. "How much do you practice a day?" He asked for a show of hands for those who practiced at least two hours, then four, then six. It was amazing the number of hands that were still proudly displayed at six hours. When he saw this, he suddenly exclaimed, "Stop it! Read a book! Go outside! Get a life!" The musicians giggled, but sat back in their chairs stunned and bewildered. They hadn't put together the idea that sitting in a practice room is not music. It is simply developing a skill. It is providing the means by which music can begin to be communicated. Life is the experience that fuels the instrumental vehicle! At the core of music is some kind of passion. If we don't embrace the human experience, do we have anything to say?

I have come to believe that we spend all those years gripping the baton—or our instrument—only to find out it was the other way around. It was the baton and all that it represents that gripped us. For whatever cosmic reason we have chosen, or have been chosen, to walk the musical path that we're on, we need to understand that at the core of what we are and do, who we are as human beings profoundly affects what we have to say. Who we are is partly determined by what we experience and by what we embrace. Do you take time to put fuel in the tank? Too busy? Perhaps the question should really be: Can you afford not to? Oh, and if you see a dark blue 1989 Isuzu Trooper on the side of the road somewhere, I'd appreciate a lift.

SIGNPOSTS

What

Taking the time for you.

When

That's completely up to you.

How

Be selfish, pure and simple. It's okay in this context. Set aside a time that is not directly related to your vocation and give yourself permission to enjoy it. Slow down. Watch. Breathe. Force yourself outside of your zone of familiarity. Again, the key is giving yourself the permission to do it. You already know what it is . . . You'll be amazed what you bring back to your art and to those you love.

THE CHIMNEY SWEEP

When I was a boy, the movie *Mary* Poppins introduced me to the chimney sweep, as played by the masterful Dick Van Dyke. In character as Bert, he was magical. He was scary. He was common and he was special, despite a horrible Cockney accent. You know that accent too, don't you? It's the one that students use when they feel like they are acting or being cute, when really...

A few of the things that especially stuck with me about Bert: He was open, he was friendly, and he had an enormous smile. Even now, decades later, watching it with my children makes *me* feel like a child again. The chimney sweep song and dance scene was one of the most fearsome things I had ever seen to that point in my short life (I saw the movie several years after its initial release on one of those cheap show weekends). Bert danced alongside a crew of other chimney sweeps: men covered in coal dust, faces hidden, clothes black, and looking very stern—all images I still carry with me when I meet with administration. They sang and danced to "Chim-Chim-Cheree," a Richard and Robert Sherman song about someone enjoying his place in the world—a place so good it was nearly contagious. "Good luck will rub off when I shake 'ands with you," they sang. Wow. How cool. And it's good to know that good luck may indeed be communicable—especially via poor hygiene.

My second chimney sweep experience came much later, in the first winter in our house in Charleston, Illinois. We had one of my most favorite things in the world: a fireplace. That house wasn't exactly a new one. In fact, when we moved in one of the students helping us remarked how everything was "so retro-1970s" and that we shouldn't change a thing. The house was older than that, but that was evidently the last update, which included blue mood lighting, blue curtains, and blue carpet to accent the living room and its large fireplace. Sometimes it's good to be colorblind.

Nowadays, fireplaces are almost purely and simply for ambience. The traditional use of a chimney, or as Slim Pickens would say: the "chimley," was not necessarily for heat, but to provide a means of allowing smoke to escape from a dwelling. In fact, that's still the most common use of a chimney. Most of the heat is lost up a chimney anyway and then there's the creosote in the chimney itself, which, when combined with wood, makes a terrific fuel. Hence, a lot of things can go wrong with a chimney in the quest for ambience, but to me, it's worth it. Since I can't flat-out build an open campfire in the house, the safest thing to do is to find a company that works, repairs, and cleans all things "chimley."

As it happened, there was just such a company that serviced Charleston. Or, should I say, one such man. And that man was a real, live, honest-to-goodness chimley sweep. My wife was so excited to call me to relay the information about a man showing up, dressed in top hat and tails, ready to take care of the chimney. Oh my gosh, Bert is for real. I had to get home as soon as possible. My son was seven years old the first time this gentleman came, so he was as intrigued as I would have been and offered to help. My son carried a bucket. He helped with tools. He bent over and turned his head to look up the chimney. In short, he was probably ready to wear that chimney sweep's "Abe Lincoln hat" as soon as possible.

I was surprised to find that this gentleman was a former teacher. He had retired from teaching and was looking for something new to occupy his time. This was the result. I could tell that there was something special about this guy. He was so patient with my son as he explained every part of what he was doing. He rewarded both my son and daughter by spraying their names on the front walk with a waterproof chemical, thereby making their names visible every time it rained. Pretty cool. I must confess that I, too, was taken with the mystique of this old profession. There was something old, simple, and wise in watching this gentleman go about his work. He was welcoming, patient, kind, gentle, and always willing to explain the process involved in whatever he was doing. What struck me most, however, was how open and friendly he was and what a big smile he had, just like my boyhood's Bert.

After he was done and it was time to go, Dick Van Dyke's voice began to fill my head again: "Good luck will rub off when I shake hands with you. Good luck will rub off when I shake hands with you." So, needing all the luck I could get, I shook his hand tightly, as did my son and daughter. Good luck will rub off, right? As I watched him drive away I couldn't help but think about our vocation and the many people we meet in it. So many. And if you think about it, every one of us is a chimney sweep. We all have something to offer, but something more than good luck. We all have something to gain from meeting and knowing others.

The Midwest Clinic in particular has to be one of the largest gatherings of "chimney sweeps" in the world! We speak about each other to each other. We form the basis for further connections through our musical pursuits, or do we? Oftentimes, we allow opportunities or chance meetings to whither. We don't see them for the open doors they are. We waste the moment. Lucky for me, I have shaken the hand of several "chimney sweeps" which provided, more than luck, a chance to turn preparedness into opportunities. Many of those opportunities provided musical insights: walking the Malvern Hills in England along the same paths trodden by Edward Elgar, eating fish and chips in the same pub frequented by Gustav Holst down by the Thames River in Hammersmith, and during masters degree work speaking with Burnett Cross, who had enormous insight into Percy Grainger and his free music machine, which Cross constructed for him. All because someone extended a hand and I shook it. Some call it networking. Some call it politics. I call it being human. We all have "good luck." We all have something to offer.

Just as important, though, is that we can all gain so much by being aware and vulnerable. But it doesn't stop with people. Every black dot on the staff paper before us presents an opportunity or "luck." Of course, luck can also be insight. Those notes often allow us to touch something deeper within ourselves. They tap into our innermost thoughts, experiences, and expectations, challenging us to understand, to communicate something more then their mere physical representation. They can make us realize something about ourselves, be reaffirming or even bring out the best we have in us. You see, in the big picture it's not simply about shaking the hand: it's about making the connection, whether it's with us, the musicians we're working with, or those we meet through our vocation. All it takes is recognizing the opportunities in front of us, whether it's through people, a possibility, or something on paper . . . and being willing to get a little ash on our hands.

SIGNPOSTS

What:

Making connections in our professional lives.

When:

At your next opportunity.

How:

1. Without limiting your choices, who would like to make contact with, if given the chance?

2. Is there something that you would like to ask the individuals you have listed?

3. Find them, whether in person, through electronic communication or phone. Introduce yourself! Offer them your name, where you're from, where you teach or study.

4. It you're able to speak with the individual in person, relax, listen, and let the conversation take its course. Again, one of the best things to do is *listen.*

5. Follow up with an e-mail or a letter. Thank the person for their time and let them know it was a pleasure to meet

them. Even if it wasn't, they still gave of their time! If you
have a follow-up question, this would be a great time to ask.

6. You have made a connection that you can tap into any time
you wish. All it takes is a reminder of your original connection as a point of reference. Quite simply, think how you
would respond and what it would take to make a connection with you and consider this when dealing with others.

7. If you meet someone at a convention, meeting, grocery
store, gym, etc., simply, introduce yourself and then follow
steps 4 through 6.

8. Good luck will rub off . . .

WALKING ON THE SHARDS

L ife happens.

Too often we forget this seemingly obvious fact in our daily teaching, learning, loving, and living. We forget that we are not always in control, and that as soon as we have made plans, life will intervene. I have a mantra I try to follow: Control is an illusion, but preparation is not. We can certainly prepare for the future, whether it pertains to a piece, a concert, our family, our life, etc., but if we think we are in control, well . . .

As performers we understand only too well. Take a look at the challenge of staging a performance. Despite careful planning, so many things can happen the day of, just minutes before, or during a performance. These include: lost part, lost score, broken instrument, sick family member, sick musician, sick conductor, snow storm, thunderstorm, tornado, no power, no sound, no lights, no administrator, no custodian, and on and on.

As music educators and conductors, we all have experienced serious and tragic matters outside of the rehearsal room that have affected matters inside our rehearsal room. I still remember vividly the day, early in my career, that I was asked to tell a student that his father had just suffered a heart attack. I can still see Mark's expression. Add to this a number of other of life's tragedies: cancer of both students and their family members; the terrible toll of answering the call of military duty and the loved ones left behind; accidents, suicides, abuse, drugs, and alcohol.

The stark reality of our profession—and of life—is that we lose students and they lose those important to them. Life happens to us and to our musicians. Because of our special relationship forged through music—which brings with it an inherent trust, confidence, and love— our musicians often turn to us for advice, help, and solace. Sometimes we can only respond with a hug and a tissue. Sometimes we can provide direction. And sometimes, the best we can do is simply be there, while our world crumbles, too.

I had been teaching at a small, rural school for three years. Years ago, the area had been a popular stop for orphan trains, whose passengers had been accepted by local families in an effort to both provide a home as well as extra hands around the farm as the children grew older. It was not always possible to keep family members together during that time and many children were taken in by different families without knowing their true familial relations due to being such a young age. This would sometimes later result in marriages of closely related bloodlines, which would then begin to produce children with slight genetic challenges. Even when I began teaching over a century after those trains had been through the area, the school district still had an unusual number of resource rooms. Incidentally, the service providers and teachers staffed in those rooms were absolutely top-notch.

A call at about 5:00 a.m. jolted me out of my sleep. It was the kind of early call that usually means something is wrong. I recognized the voice of a fellow faculty member and close friend. She told me to listen to everything she had to say. "Milt," she said. "Lillie was killed last night."

I was waiting for the punch line.

It never came.

Lillie was twelve years old. She was one of my seventh graders and a star clarinetist. Even more, she was *that* kid: mature beyond her years, with the wisdom to match. All the other band members were drawn to her and they followed her lead both inside and outside of the class. She was always happy, didn't care what other kids thought, and was always kind and considerate. She was known for always standing up for those who were picked on. She was also a great student.

But she was only twelve. And she had died.

It still wasn't completely registering. I must still be dreaming, I thought. I asked my colleague what had happened.

One of Lillie's friends was an older boy named John. I knew John, because part of my assigned duties included serving as detention supervisor and John was a frequent guest. His father had left years before and he and his siblings had been raised by his mother. He was learning disabled with a variety of social problems that made him an easy target for his classmates. His I.Q. registered just four points above the line considered "mentally handicapped" at the time. He was known for his temper outbursts and also for his stark honesty. John possessed the capacity for great compassion. He seemed to be a caring kid, one who would open up to me about his treatment, feelings, and hopes, as well as his disappointments and anger. He needed a friend, so I tried to simply give him an ear when I could, both in detention and in greeting him when I saw him in the hall.

Lillie, as it turned out, did the same. She lived near John and was always good to him, although he was six years her senior. She wasn't afraid to call John a friend and helped him when she could. This was what led to the evening that changed lives forever.

My friend explained what happened as I sat dazed on the edge of my bed, barely able to hold the phone. John had returned home the previous night with blood all over his clothes, and said it was from skinning catfish—a common occurrence in the small river town. John's mother had heard that Lillie had not returned home from a ride on her moped and that members and friends of Lillie's family, along with law enforcement officials, were searching the area, trying to find her. John joined the search, then after some questioning, made a shocking confession: the blood on his clothes was Lillie's.

He had killed her.

Riddled with guilt and remorse, John gave a recorded confession, a written confession, and then a videotaped tour of the crime scene. According to his account, Lillie had offered him a ride home on her new moped. He accepted. As they were riding, John attempted to fondle Lillie. She stopped the moped and chastised him, sending him into a rage. In his own words, he "freaked out." He dragged her into some nearby brush where he choked her into unconsciousness and sexually assaulted her. Beginning to understand the magnitude of his actions, he feared getting beat up at school as well as going to jail. His solution was to beat her to death with a fence post, stand on her neck, then drag her lifeless form over some railroad tracks in hopes that a train would run her over, providing an alibi.

I was now fully awake and crying.

Lillie . . .

John . . .

After the call, I got up quickly, dressed, and headed to school to help comfort those students who came to school that day as well as to be with the other teachers. What I hadn't counted on, though, was the media. Radio and television stations had been monitoring the various emergency radio frequencies and were following what was happening. Before students had even arrived at school, the media swarmed to this first- through twelfth-grade campus and set up shop, waiting for the busses to pull in. The majority of the faculty still did not know what had happened. None of the students, except those from Lillie and John's little town, knew either. The entire school, then, was caught completely unprepared as well as uninformed on how to handle the situation. As I pulled into the school's fenced-in compound, I could see that media vans lined the entire pull-through drive in front of the middle school, poised to scoop the story. I saw no teachers, nor any other personnel who might have been present to help the situation. It wasn't till much later in the day that additional counselors were available. Essentially, we were on our own and most of us, teachers and students, still didn't know the news.

As the first busses started to arrive, I stood by myself in front of the middle school and watched the students through the bus windows, excitedly pointing at the vans. Reporters with cameras and microphones rushed to catch the first utterance of the students as they came off the bus. But the students didn't know what had happened, and for the ten- through twelve-year-olds coming off the bus, the news of Lillie's death was delivered in a careless and shocking question: "How do you feel about your friend being killed?" I will never forget seeing those kids.

My students.

Our students.

Sons, daughters, brothers, and sisters.

I had seen some beautiful things in my life. Profound things, too, as well as things that seemed to rise from a dark place—but nothing had ever come close to watching the innocence leave those children as the media broke the news to them. I was an unwilling spectator, watching childhood end as they encountered the stark reality of how fragile life is. I tried to stop the cameras and the microphones, but there just weren't many of us there yet. It was a total and uncontrolled media heyday. I tried to comfort students as they came into the school, crying. I watched some of the bravest teachers I've ever seen fight their own emotions to be there for those students. Every teacher was a hero that day. And every student needed one.

The faculty gathered during planning periods and tried to comfort each other. Parents came throughout the day and took kids home. Everyone tried to make sense out of something that was senseless. Somehow, with shattered hearts, we made it through that day. Some teachers were to later leave the district to teach elsewhere, the recollection of that day just too difficult to shoulder. Other teachers would completely leave teaching, unable to cope with what happened.

The next day, I went to visit Lillie's mom just to let her know that I was there and thinking about the family. As I drove up to the small house, front yard littered with toys, I couldn't help but imagine the place in happier times. I rounded the house and knocked on the back door. A friend of the family let me in. As she went to get Lillie's mother, I saw Lillie's little sister playing in the living room. She ran up to me and in a rural Missouri drawl announced, "Lillie's day-yed."

I focused on the picture she had drawn and was holding up for me to see. It was an angel with a full gown on, complete with glowing halo. Even though the artist was only four or five years old, you could still recognize Lillie's hair, eyes, and smile through the crayons. "She's going to be with God in heaven." I couldn't speak. I didn't know what to say anyway. What do you say?

Lillie's mom came out. It was clear she hadn't slept since Lillie's disappearance and that she had been crying nonstop. She was tired and she was lost. Again, I didn't know what to say, choosing to be silent rather than saying the wrong thing, so we simply held on to each other and cried for a bit together. It was then I had a memory from a Christmas long ago.

When I was little, we always had glass Christmas ornaments. One Christmas one of those ornaments fell on our hard, wood floor as we decorated the tree. It smashed into what seemed like hundreds of piec-es. I was barefoot and I remember my mom telling us not to move. She said she needed to sweep up the glass or we would step on the glass shards no matter where we stepped. They were small, too. So small that we wouldn't be able to see them until we stepped on them and cut our feet. "Stay still," she said. "Don't move until you're told it's alright." And now, here I was again, shards all around me from something beautiful that had fallen and shattered, once again not knowing what to do and waiting for someone to tell me it would be all right, but it wasn't just me. There was a family, a faculty, a student body, and a community: all trying not to walk on the shards, but to no avail. We were all cut and bloodied in varying degrees.

Lillie's funeral was open-casket. The family thought it best to let those who needed to see her one last time to be able to do so. The funeral home had done the best they could to make her look presentable after what had been done to her. Still, it didn't seem like her. She lay there in her favorite dress, uncharacteristically motionless. We waited for the joke to be on us, but she never did sit up. It was a hard service. John, meanwhile, was put on suicide watch and had to be covered when escorted to and from the courthouse for fear of retribution. His family was receiving hateful phone calls, death threats, and all other manner of harassment and intimidation. It was hard to remember that two families, not just one, were changed forever by what had happened. Both families were suffering and grieving.

At a special memorial ceremony open to the entire school, students and faculty were allowed to express their feelings and remember Lillie in some way. I spoke as to how fortunate we were to have had her in our lives and that she would always be a part of us. Still, I was walking on shards. John would later be sentenced to life in prison without the possibility of parole. The death sentence was avoided because of John' mental incapacities. I had been called to testify on Lillie's behalf, but wasn't selected to do so. Perhaps it was because I knew John too well. Perhaps it was because there was a larger truth that had gnawed at me since the tragedy unfolded.

While John was in school, faculty had encouraged the administration to find a suitable placement for John where he could receive the special treatment he needed. But the small school district, with a limited budget, chose not to take the recommendation because of the fiscal impact it would have. I felt Lillie paid the price for that decision, and right or wrong, I felt the school was an accomplice in her murder because it paved the way for the inevitability as a result of its decision. I realize that this is a brash and perhaps unreasonable conclusion. Good people administered that school. Great people, but I couldn't recon-cile the results any other way. So, I was one of those teachers who left the classroom. I quit. I left. I couldn't face the idea that the very insti-tution that I worked at and supported could contribute to what had happened.

Over the course of the next year, I not only left teaching, but music as well. I wanted as far away from the rehearsal hall as possible. I had a lot of thinking to do about who I was, what I was, and what I was sup-posed to do and be. I had never been more lost.

During that year, I spoke with a few of my old mentors. One in particular encouraged me to continue teaching. He talked about my responsibility to the profession, to students, and to the music. He had always been one of the most important musical figures and mentors in my life, and I thought long and hard about what he told me and encouraged me to do. I realized that I wasn't "finished" with music and teaching; I was simply running. I was running from my responsibilities, my talents, my soul, and my element. It was time to get back to doing what made me happiest: making music and trying to help others dis-cover the power of music in their lives.

In a strange way, I owe that to Lillie. Had it not been for what hap-pened to her, I may have never faced some extremely difficult self-spec-ulation. I may have never really thought about my vocation. And so it was, after walking on the shards of a broken life, it was music's voice that finally said it was all right to move. There are many colleagues who have experienced similar tragedies in their lives. Those tragedies some-times force our backs to the wall, forcing us to determine what is truly important in our lives. This ordeal was one of the most important, life-changing events to have shaped me. Did I recover? I don't think one ever does, but I do think somehow, in our own way, we come to peace with such events. Since I've returned to teaching I've never looked back, but I look up when I can. Lillie wasn't just a great student, but one of the best teachers I've ever had.

How have you dealt with loss and your musicians or how might you deal with it?

RATTLESNAKES

There are a lot of rattlesnakes in South Dakota. A lot.

In particular, there are a lot of rattlesnakes on the Cheyenne River Sioux Reservation. Now, you may not be a snake lover, but realize that most snakes aren't human lovers, either. Yet, the Lakota people consider the rattlesnake our brother and part of the proof is in the rattle. The Lakota people believe that because rattlesnakes care about us, they let us know if we are near them or if we're about to step on them.

I am one of those people who had always been fascinated by snakes. I was also one of those kids who was initially petrified by snakes. I'd see a snake and my voice would communicate with my legs in some kind of language that sounded like a ghost with a bad, descending vibrato. My legs would then take that cue and turn and run. During all of this, my rational mind would take a back seat and simply enjoy the show.

As I grew older, I caught snakes and became more comfortable around them. Bull snakes, garter snakes, and ring-necks were the snakes of choice where I grew up. Oh, sure, I'd dream of an encounter with something poisonous and huge with rattles. Eventually the rattle-less but poisonous and cranky Osage Copperhead would become quite familiar, but it was on the rez that I finally came face to face on

106

a regular basis with rattlers. Next think I knew, I'd become the official "how not to get bitten by snakes that visitors can't even recognize" guy for all visiting work/college groups to the Sioux YMCA in Dupree. Groups would come volunteer for anywhere from a few days to several weeks during spring breaks and summers.

It was the summer session that I was helping get ready, which included setting up the teepee camp by the Missouri River—prime rattlesnake country. You know it's serious rattlesnake country when even the locals tell you not to go in the dried-up creek beds fingering from the river. Setting up camp involved building, fencing (often done in tall grass), collecting trash, and other duties. The facilities in general were intentionally primitive. This meant that one had to constantly be aware of where and how one walked.

South Dakota's only native venomous snake, the prairie rattlesnake (*crotalus viridis viridis*), is a subspecies of the western rattlesnake (*crotalus viridis*). Its color varies from light brown to green, with a yellowish belly. It has blotches on its back, which appear as cross bands of sorts. Adults will range from thirty to forty inches up to a record fifty-seven inches. A three-footer will weigh in at about one pound, while the record stands at just over four and a half pounds.

Contrary to popular belief, a snake cannot launch itself at its prey. In fact, it can only strike about half the total length of its body. If it works out a lot, attends frequent Pilates classes, and has a very strong core and good lower body muscles, it might even get close to two-thirds, but that would probably be a snake Olympic record. Most people, though, still believe that a snake can magically grow several feet, sprout wings, and fly, which is actually a healthy belief. Remember, we're talking about a living, thinking, poisonousssss, hypodermic needle that essentially lives to kill things so it can eat and make baby poisonous hypodermic needles. It's definitely good to err on the side of caution here.

Snakes are deaf and have poor eyesight, though they can sense vibration. A snake will use its tongue—a *bifurcated* or forked tongue—to sense the air, gather those molecules, and transfer the information to the Jacobson's organ on the roof of its mouth, where it senses a combination of smell and taste. The forked tongue can also sense heat, which enables the snake to sense movement. A *moving* heat source usually means *food*, or perhaps something big and threatening. So, boys and girls, let's be careful about putting our hands and feet in places we can't see: These appendages appear to our little brother as potential food!

To that end, here are some things I have found helpful to remember when in snake country, especially rattlesnake country, but please remember: I am not a licensed medical doctor and what follows are guidelines! Read a book or talk to a medical doctor to be sure. As a licensed musical doctor I can, however, tell what key a snake is in, their harmonic structure, etc. So here you go . . .

1. Remember you're in their home. They will protect it.
2. Watch where you walk.
3. Don't stick your hand in a place/rock/shelf/etc. that you can't see. Use a stick instead. Or someone you don't like.
4. Don't act like a rodent at any time. (This is also degrading to rodents.)
5. Move rocks and logs with a stick or something long.
6. Stomp on sheets of wood, or shake tarps before removing. If you hear a rattle . . .

7. If you see a rattler, then perhaps you might choose another path.

8. If you see a snake very, very close, and you're not sure you can walk away, FREEZE. DON'T MOVE. Movement is what they need to find you.

9. If you hear a rattle, FREEZE. You may want to begin praying, too. Hard. (Remember, snakes with no rattles don't give you this chance; they are the genus *jerkus snakus no warningus*.)

10. If you have been bitten, do not bleed the wound, contrary to popular belief. If you do, you will cause the poison to work faster. Keep calm (seriously), restrict movement, keep the affected area below heart level, removing anything that may impede swelling near the bitten area, i.e. clothing, belts, rings. If someone killed the snake, carefully bring it along as you GET THEE TO A HOSPITAL ASAP (especially if you're not sure if it's poisonous or nonpoisonous, although those two fang marks are pretty telling).

11. Remind yourself that only about ten people die per year in the United States from poisonous snakebite.

An aside, nonpoisonous snakebites are simply a bit scary and annoying. Scary because, hey, it's a snake, and annoying because the teeth end up being like little splinters that you'll probably be needing some tweezers to pull out. That, my friends, is the voice of experience.

So, there I am during that summer with a group from Kansas City working on the camp. I had to make a run into the nearest town for some building supplies, food, and water. It was getting very late by the time one of the group's sponsors and I were heading back on West Highway 12. Dusk and night are both interesting snake times on the res. It's not unusual to see rattlers stretched out along the warm roads, seeking respite from the quickly cooling air. One such snake, a big'un over forty inches, was stretched out on the road as we passed. It was magnificent.

My friend was instantly petrified. I tried to calm him by telling him there were no recorded instances of anyone ever being bit through a car or truck while driving by a snake of any kind. Of course, I did add the word "yet" at the end.

Dumb.

Still, sensing a teachable moment, I pulled the truck over and mentioned to the KC sponsor next to me, "Hey, wanna take a look at this live one?" To which he promptly and firmly replied, "NO." I again explained to him that snakes could not fly, we would be safely away from the animal, and I would make sure that nothing was in the ditch (which didn't help him much). He finally consented and we ventured outside of the truck . . . a good twenty-five feet from the snake. I was leaning against the truck, and my cohort had climbed from the cab of the truck into the bed without touching the ground. He still didn't feel too safe even then, expecting the snake to approach with lightning speed, biting me, and then getting to him. Cars zoomed by and we watched this beautiful animal until one of the passing cars ran over its back. Now, a snake that cannot slither is going to die a slow and miserable death. Keep in mind that the front three-quarters still worked fine, but it was obvious that this critter's days were numbered.

During our observation, one of the local ranchers had driven up to watch, too. An older Lakota man, he knew of me and figured I was up to something. We quickly discussed that the snake needed to be put out of its misery. A noble creature, it needed to die with honor. That's when the idea came to me. We would put the snake out of its misery, then I would throw it in the back of the truck and take it back to camp to show the other volunteers not only what the rattlers in our area looked like, but what they felt like, what they smelled like, even what their fangs looked like. In its death, it would be a teacher. Oh yes, I had a plan— but no means of dispatching the snake. My Lakota neighbor solved that problem with a scoop shovel and several whacks to the snake's head.

It didn't comfort my companion any that, before dispatching of our slithering animal, my Lakota friend had the snake strike the shovel (at my request) so that this volunteer could see and hear the predator in action. I mean, how often does the opportunity present itself with no aquarium glass standing between man and reptile? Well, after the fatal blow, the snake was scooped up and thrown into the truck bed . . . where the volunteer was. What I found truly amazing was that, some-how, the human in the truck bed suddenly disappeared from the back of the pickup and reappeared in the truck cab in the time it took the dead snake to leave the scoop shovel and "thud" onto the back of the truck bed. He was still holding his breath when I jumped into the cab. I guess I should have told him that we were going to throw the snake into the back of the truck.

Off we went to camp, snake not breathing, volunteer not breath-ing, and me trying to keep my big mouth shut by not adding any more perspective to the situation.

It was a bit after midnight when we arrived at the small village where the volunteers stayed before moving to the camp. My fellow adventurer was right on my heels as I walked into the small house, still looking back at the truck, waiting for the snake to suddenly become ani-mated and rocket toward us. I casually, coolly announced to the rest of the volunteers that the supplies were in the back of the truck, but "mind the rattler." I felt like I needed to give them some kind of warning since there weren't laundry facilities close by. It did take a few moments for those words to sink in. But when they did, oh my, was there a reaction. First, everyone froze as though the rattler was in the room, a moment that I was particularly proud of, since they had obviously listened to my snake talk. I told them the snake was not in the house, but in the bed of the truck, dead. I explained what had happened and that they now had an opportunity to see, touch, and experience a rattler first hand without the challenge of dealing with a fully interactive model.

They exploded out of the house toward the truck.

By the time I got to the truck parked on the road just beyond the small front yard, the entire group of volunteers had already excitedly grouped around the bed, though about fifteen feet behind. I walked through this group of twelve and grabbed the tailgate latch, opened it with a quick flip, and let the tailgate drop open to form a desk, of sorts, to work with. The moon glowed off of the snake's back as a collective sucking of air came from the group. It was suddenly quiet as the stars shown down on this silent teacher. The carcass had slid forward toward the cab in the truck's large bed, so I grabbed a long stick to reach it and then slide it toward me. The nervous crowd inched forward to see the snake and listen to my descriptions and explanations. I could now reach this lifeless, scaly rope easily and put the stick down. "Note the *scales*," I said, a musical pun that only I appreciated. "See the blotch pattern? The pits to enable sensing heat, here behind the head?"

And then I heard something. Something primeval. A sound that seemed to trigger my old ghost voice, though I kept that voice quiet now. It was a rattle. In the time it took my eyes to look at my feet, thinking another snake had gone under the warm truck, my mind realized with great concern what my ears were truly hearing: the sound was coming from the truck bed.

The rattlesnake wasn't dead.

Instantly, I removed my hand from its head. This seemed a prudent move. No sooner had I done this than it gathered its remaining body together into a coil, readying to strike. I instantly and dutifully froze and examined the situation. I noticed, obviously, that the rattler was pretty banged up. It was swaying a bit like a cobra, not coiled firmly like it should be. It was clear that it was on its last "leg," but still in working order. I could see in the moonlight the bifurcated tongue flicking, but coming out of the snake's mouth at a forty-degree angle: It wasn't tracking accurately! Talk about a New York minute, lasting only a second or three.

The group behind me, upon hearing the rattles, became, shall we say, quite excited. I quickly asked them to be quiet. They did so and froze. So there we were—me, them, and a really cranky rattlesnake with a broken back, sore mouth, and ringing concussion. It was within this split second, just as everyone was relaxing, that it happened: The rattler struck. And missed me. Those whacks on the head had not only caused problems with the tongue, but perhaps a few slipped discs as well. Regardless, it struck at me, but missed just slightly for two reasons: 1) It couldn't strike accurately, and 2) I'd like to think that I maintained the distance rule. It was after the strike, though, that the real excitement occurred.

The volunteer group right behind me absolutely and completely disintegrated into a screaming, running mob. It was as though someone hit a button. I mean, they went from total calm into what appeared like a piranha feeding frenzy, except they weren't feeding. They were running for their lives. It looked like those films of people the day after Christmas when the big store opens its doors for those giant sales. Except those shoppers don't have panic and survival written all over their faces. I remember hearing an enormous bang, then a ringing sound, but didn't think much of it. In the meantime, I quickly pinned the rattler on the truck bed as it was trying to slither away, took my knife out, and quickly cut its head off, putting it out of its misery once and for all.

It took ten to fifteen minutes before we located most of the volunteers. Several ran down the road, which wasn't the smartest thing to do in a one-road, unlit village on a dark night in rattlesnake country. A couple had jumped into the truck cab. We rounded everyone up and went into the house where the rest had sought shelter. Everything was settling down, the rattler was dispatched, nobody bit and nobody hurt. Or so I thought. Turns out we were still missing two people: one sponsor and one volunteer.

I heard my name being hollered, so I went back to the front yard. My fellow "adventurer" sponsor came walking up to me with one of the college-aged volunteers whose face was covered in blood. My first thought was, "How did the snake bite her face, let alone produce this much blood?" Then, I saw the gash. It stretched across the bridge of her nose at a forty-five-degree angle and it was a beauty. Without question, we were looking at stitches and I figured these sutures were going to be a bit out of my league. It was instantly clear that while we had dodged one obvious trip to the emergency room, we weren't going to do so this time. But, how did this happen? What could possibly make this kind of gash? Had she fallen on a rock? Brick? Ran into someone during the melee of survival? It was none of the above. She had been attacked.

By the dumpster.

I thought back to that bang/ringing sound I had heard. In her uncontrolled fear and reaction, she had turned and run with abandon as fast as her legs would carry her . . . right into one of only a handful of dumpsters in the entire village. Aaaaagh. So, back in the truck with the sponsor and this unfortunate but no less cheerful young lady for the almost-two-hour trip to the emergency room. During the ride, she realized that her fears of the rattler were basically unfounded, if for no other reason than proximity. She was at the back of the group, probably twenty feet from the reptile, when the action occurred. She simply reacted without thinking and followed that up with running towards anywhere. Anywhere, in this case, ended up being the hospital off the reservation in Gettysburg, South Dakota ("Where the Battle Wasn't," according to the town's sign).

Teachable moment, indeed.

Now, I'm fairly sure at this point that you may be enjoying this little tale, but wondering what in the world it has to do with music? Well, let's take a look back at those rules. In fact, let's translate them a bit to "our" world. Let us also imagine that rattlesnake as a potential professional or personal threat or challenge while remembering it's us who choose to view something or someone in that way, whether it's accurate or not . . .

SIGNPOSTS

What:

Managing potential professional, musical, or personal challenges.

When:

Today!

How:

Let's take a look back at those "rules." In fact, let's translate them a bit to "our" world. Imagine that "rattlesnake" as a potential professional, musical or personal threat or challenge. Remember: It's we who choose to view something or someone in any specific way, whether it's accurate or not. Now for that review . . .

1. Remember you're in their home. They will protect it.

   Whether it's another state, school, festival, contest, event, or meeting, always respect the given locale and accompanying beliefs, tendencies, or agendas thereof.

2. Watch where you walk.

   Quite simply, is something truly your business? Is it something that will affect the education of your musicians? Is it something that affects you in some way that prevents you from being who you really are or what you really want to be?

3. Don't stick your hand in a place/rock/shelf/etc. that you can't see. Use a stick instead. Or someone you don't like.

   Whether it's making accusations or insights toward something we really don't have all the facts on, or even making score decisions when we really haven't done the work to infer composer intent, making assumptions often causes problems. We are best left to things we understand and acknowledge those areas that are new to us and, in some cases, needing further study.

4. Don't act like a rodent at any time. (This is also degrading to rodents.)

   Remain professional, but also remain true to who and what you are. By the way, let the students act like students . . .

5. Move rocks and logs with a stick or something long.

6. Stomp on sheets of wood, or shake tarps before removing. If you hear a rattle . . .

   Many times it's best to "test the waters." Perhaps we're trying repertoire with our students, or thinking about pursuing that advanced degree. Maybe we're considering a large program change like adding another ensemble or a complete curriculum revamp. It's important that we gather the facts, ask those we trust for advice, and consider the long-term repercussions. If we choose to act without thinking, then we choose to accept the consequences of our actions. But remember: Sometimes a little reckless abandon isn't all bad!

7. If you see a rattler, then perhaps you might choose another path.

   You may see a problem in a person. You may have a mental block in your score study. You may not be able to figure a way to accomplish what you are trying in the current direction you're curriculum dictates. If so, go a different direction! Try something from a different perspective! Use a different technique! Just remember that sometimes you don't need to go the complete opposite direction, you simply need to "walk around" the problem.

8. If you see a snake very, very close, and you're not sure you can walk away, FREEZE. DON'T MOVE. Movement is what they need to find you.

9. If you hear a rattle, FREEZE. You may want to begin praying, too. Hard. (Remember, snakes with no rattles don't give you this chance; they are the genus *jerkus snakus no warningus*.)

   When we encounter challenges, sometimes the best thing to do is not react, not say the first thing that comes to mind, not formulate an immediate response. The best thing to do could very well be to wait, to be patient, and thoughtfully consider all possibilities. Action may require reaction, but it doesn't have to be immediate.

10. If you are bitten, *do not* bleed the wound, as what used to be the case. If you do, you will cause the poison to work faster. Keep calm (seriously), restrict movement, keep the affected area *below* heart level, removing anything that may impede swelling near the bitten area, i.e. clothing, belts, rings. If someone killed the snake, carefully bring it along as you GET THEE TO A HOSPITAL ASAP (especially if you're not sure if it's poisonous or nonpoisonous, although those two fang marks are pretty telling).

When things happen, breathe. Do not gossip, do not tell the next teacher or student, do not become a human megaphone, announcing the situation. Oftentimes, this confounds a given situation. If possible, keep things from escalating by remembering to regard it as an isolated situation and treat as such when possible. Speak directly with the administrator, teacher, student, supporter, or whomever is involved directly. Or, perhaps you simply need to let that score lay on the desk a bit. Or maybe you need to go get a cup of coffee and sit on a bench you haven't sat on while you give yourself a chance to think a little bit.

View things as situational, as objective. When we attach a subjective evaluation, we often lose our ability to reason.

11. Remind yourself that only about ten people die per year in the United States from poisonous snakebite.

    What we do, by and large, doesn't result in death. Just something to keep in perspective.

If You Build It . . .

As a band, we were small. So small that we made every other "small" band look big. In a Catholic high school of 110 students, we had seven students in the high school band when I took over the program—and that ain't a high school band. That's a septet. Three trumpets, one alto sax, one horn/mellophone, and two trombones. We occasionally had a bari sax, too. Thus began the process of rebuilding a program in shambles.

So what to do? Well, it was obvious that there was a pretty serious problem with numbers, which I was sure hinged on quality of the group (which it did) and the resulting school perception that the band wasn't good (which I'll get to), and the fact that sports, especially football, were an extremely dominant part of the school (as they are in most small schools).

The approximately eighty-member junior high school was housed in the same building and that summer prior to my tenure beginning, I was able to recruit to get the junior high band to twenty-eight members and, with some trust and instrument switching, didn't have too bad an instrumentation. Still, my flagship group, the high school band, had a serious educational problem, not to mention identity complex.

One thing was clear: We would not be performing the Hindemith *Symphony in B-flat.*

All during that summer prior to my first year at this school, I had researched the school and the program. The band had a once-proud tradition both on the marching field and especially in the concert hall. They had been a source of pride for the school and the community (which boasted two other high schools with enrollments of around twelve hundred each), and were recognized statewide. Okay, so I had that going for me.

I researched the band director lineage going back to the opening of the school in the 1920s. I followed that lineage as well as the school enrollment, band instrumentation, curriculum changes, and successes. It was clear that as sports became a stronger part of the school, the band program suffered, but only because of what appeared to be a combination of lack of quality music making and the seeming expertise of the person in charge at the time. In other words, there wasn't a noticeable correlation between the rise of mini-dynasties in football, basketball, volleyball, softball, and baseball, and the decline of the band. What seemed to correlate more directly was the effect each different director had on the program. The "woe is me" argument didn't hold water here. What clearly did was the quality of teaching and music making as well as the commitment and expertise of the person on the podium.

Over the summer, I had called students no longer enrolled in band and begged them back, while also asking them about their previous band experience. I spoke with area band directors, mentors, parents, teachers, students, and the local music store folks, all to help me understand the community, the extracurricular role the band had played, and what had been happening with the curriculum and the role of *music* itself. I acquainted myself with people and resources that I thought might assist me with the program as well as help spread the word that something exciting was brewing at the school.

Finally, I formulated "The Plan": my goal for the program and how I was going to accomplish it. I spoke with the administration about expectations and had them review "The Plan." I told them that one thing was clear: Music and music education at the school had lost its stature years before and that the role of the band program now, from junior high to high school, was reduced to providing entertainment at sports events.

"The Plan" began with a statement of philosophy, supported by a mission statement, a purpose statement, and, lastly, an outcomes statement. I had tied these into school, state, and national standards, all things the administration wasn't aware of. I then provided an introduction that explained the role of music education in general and what I thought the role of the band program in particular should be in our school.

It is important to note that I was hired to fix the problem of an embarrassing band program. In other words, the band didn't sound or look good at athletic functions. The fact that very little was happening in the rehearsal room seemed of little consequence, but I didn't blame the administration. It takes time to change a culture and the administration had been led to believe that the role of the band was mainly as a supporter of the athletic teams, with a little music education thrown in, because that sounded, well, politically correct. But let's face it. When, at a school football game, a priest and a bishop forbid the playing of the national anthem by the local Catholic school's band on the grounds that it is unrecognizable, then something has gone musically haywire.

The *priest* and the *bishop*? That almost equates to God coming down and saying: "*That* was supposed to be the national anthem? Okay, that's it. Stop it."

So on I went, explaining The Plan, fully expecting to be fired at any moment before the school year even started, by a principal who not only openly claimed to know nothing about music, but who also looked like an ex-NFL lineman. One of the first objectives I put forth was that I was going to separate the high school and junior high band programs, which had been joined some years back in order to provide a marching band for football games. Talk about the tail wagging the dog. Actually, talk about a stubby, broken, and emaciated tail wagging a hellhound.

It was, in fact, my decision that led to the high school "septet." I proposed that we split the high school "band" from the middle school band. I did that partly to give the high school band program a separate identity, and partly to more appropriately meet the needs of all the students. When I did it, I knew that it would either be a major step toward salvaging a sunken ship, or it would mean a quick exit by yours truly.

This was definitely the first big test with my principal. I explained the idea, sat back in my chair, stared at the picture of Christ just above my administrator's head, and waited to be fired. But he didn't fire me. In fact, he supported me completely and asked me to let him know what he could do to help. I couldn't help but notice that Christ was smiling in the picture. I told the principal that I would like to have a meeting this summer for all parents interested in finding out about the changes in the program. They could certainly bring their students, but I knew to make the kind of changes I was looking would need the support of the parents first. Of course, I would need the music booster board to support The Plan as well. He agreed to such a parent meeting and arranged to get communication sent out. Prior to that, however, I still needed to speak with the booster board members and get their first reaction to a pretty radical, sudden reformation of the program. I was nervous.

I prepared handouts, a PowerPoint presentation, and even took a shower (!) in preparation for the music booster board meeting. I had been keeping the booster president in the loop and I knew that she was extremely supportive, so that put me at ease a bit. When I distributed the handouts, quiet fell on the room like a ton of bricks. I began to explain The Plan while glancing at body language. Initially, all eyes were on the handouts. There was no other movement. I couldn't even hear breathing. Slowly, the board members began to relax a bit. Fingers tapped. Feet shifted. Some leaned back in their chairs while holding the document in front of them. Then, one by one, they began to glance up. They were looking at each other, probably, I figured, to determine who was going to tell me to go pack my things. Finally, one of them spoke. "I didn't even know that we weren't meeting school and state criteria, let alone that there are standards," one mom said. "I didn't know there were standards either, you know, like a real class," another offered. The lone male on the board responded, "Are we in violation of state codes? Is the school in trouble?" And on and on they went. With unanimous support, it was time to go public with The Plan.

As I walked into the library for the BIG public meeting a few weeks later, I looked around. I was pleased to see that it was standing room only, with both junior high and high school parents attending. There were a few students there as well. I passed out the handouts just prior to beginning the presentation, hoping to stave off anyone from running away early. PowerPoint on, game face on, principal present, I launched into The Plan. I provided the same philosophical statements as I did to the administration and the booster board. Then, I proceeded to Scary Part No. 1: acknowledging that the program was indeed in need of repair or, rather, resurrection—something this Catholic school was well acquainted with.

I knew that this would be difficult. Alliances run deep in any program, as deep as individual perceptions of experience. I was careful to never place blame on the preceding director, but put forth what I felt were glaring problems with the current program. I began with the following statements, focusing on the imbalanced current role of the band:

The core of any excellent/educationally sound band program is the concert band class itself. While it is recognized that the band plays an important part in school and community service, it is important to remember that the first priority of any band class is that of music education. Performances, contests, and concerts are certainly a part of the successful music education experience, but not at the expense of students' quality of instruction. There must be a healthy balance of curricular and extracurricular activities for effective instruction to occur.

For several years previous, [school] has combined the junior and senior high bands for performances, basically relegating the band program's function to that of simply a school spirit organization at the expense of appropriate music education.

I knew that these statements could have caused a lot of "discussion," so I didn't waste time going further down the path of sure position removal. I called a spade a spade. I listed the current problems of the program based on what I had observed or discovered:

- lack of performance quality
- inappropriate literature for both junior and senior high school levels
- student dropout due to lack of quality
- misnomers about student participation in sports, forensics debate, etc.
- elimination of a viable middle training program between elementary and senior high school-poor school and community perception

I waited for either open mutiny or gunshots, and then went on.

It is my intention to separate the junior and senior high programs to:

- *provide an appropriate music education for students at respective levels*
- *empower each band (junior and senior) as independent units*
- *to re-establish vertical articulation in the band program*

It was now very quiet. Very, very quiet. Awkward quiet. The kind of quiet in which you expect something to happen very quickly and very loudly. But, mercifully, the onslaught never came. Even more amazing was that nobody left the room. I continued to explain The Plan, which included the "suspension of the marching program" in favor of a simple stand-band for athletic events. This would also allow the separation of the junior and senior high bands while establishing a vertical articulation and corresponding curriculum.

Of course, I wanted to make the high school experience a bit more active in terms of performances and opportunities, which included athletic band performances. In this way, the middle school students could concentrate on performance experiences more appropriate to their level as well as provide me the educational opportunity to be much more selective about those performances. I went on to explain more plan objectives and then realistically outlined what specific current challenges there were to providing a successful implementation of not just The Plan, but providing a terrific music education experience:

- appropriate structure and curriculum
- student enrollment numbers
- instrumentation and inventory

Neither level of band had appropriate instrumentation due to lack of members. This was a good thing, because if we had solid membership, I would have had to figure out a way to provide instruments like bassoons, oboes, horns, trombones, baritones, tubas, and—get this—an entire concert band percussion section. There was no concert percussion to be found. Not a bass drum, a snare drum, xylophone, timpani—anything. This would have been especially difficult since my annual budget was five hundred dollars . . . for everything. Consumables, instruments, music, and repair: whatever.

My agreement with the administration was that as I began to retain students, I would provide a three-year projection of possible needs based on growth over that time. The school did have a few things: one drum set, two clarinets (donated by nuns thirty years prior), two bari saxes (?), and my personal favorite, a Mirafone tuba. Kind of like dressing a pig in a tuxedo. There were a few other instruments, but they were clearly beyond repair and pronounced deceased by our terrific local music store. I sent them to that big band room in the sky in a quick ceremony at dumpster #2 behind the school. I finished my explanation of The Plan by pointing out the positives toward accomplishing The Plan:

- supportive administration
- supportive parent group

- quality instructor
- students who want to achieve

I concluded the presentation by inviting any interested students to feel free to contact me and made it clear that I understood that this band was not for everybody. It was going to take hard, hard work and a tremendous amount of dedication, but those who would join me would be a part of something very special.

Many parents spoke with me afterword, explaining that they wholeheartedly supported the changes, but that they didn't think that they could cajole their students to participate again. I didn't mind. Why? Because the musical culture of that school had already started to change. There was a sense of excitement and promise in the air and I knew that I had to have that in order to face the challenges ahead. I still only ended up with seven enrolled in the high school band, but we were off and running. Well, kind of.

The first day of class was the only time I could get the all students together. My first task was to build both the self-esteem of the high school band and its perception within the school and community. The key was a quality musical experience first and foremost. If I could establish rehearsal and performance expectations with honest input from the students, we had a shot. So, on the first day of class, I reiterated my plan with the high school band members. All seven of them. Knowing that honest self-evaluation is an important part of growth, I asked them what they thought the school perception of the high school band was. They were silent. They looked at each other. I was sensing that we might have a problem with obvious reality. Then, finally, one of them spoke:

"Can I use kind of a bad word?"

I didn't see this coming in a parochial school, but I sensed that this might not only be a moment of gaining trust, but also a teachable moment.

"Sure, as long as it's not something you wouldn't say to a priest."

"Okay," one of my two trombonists went on. "The school thinks we suck."

Wanting to remain positive and really wanting to understand what they felt about themselves, I quickly responded, "Okay, that's what the school thinks, but what do *you* all think?"

And then it happened. The response was honest, accurate, and succinct.

"Well . . . we suck!"

I was elated. They "sucked!" *And they knew it*! This was extremely important and the real beginning of turning the program around. If the response had been, "We're good" or "We're great" or worse yet, "We don't care," then I knew I would have had a serious problem. Metacognition is so important for individual growth, let alone for a music ensemble. It's sometimes very difficult to accurately and honestly assess one's skill level in anything in order to progress. These students, however, couldn't have been more accurate, or more honest. They did "suck." Big time. They knew it and I knew it and the eight-hundred-pound gorilla in the room was noticed. I knew, too, that my response was going to be extremely important, so after the briefest of pauses, I countered, "No problem! Maybe we can get Hoover vacuum cleaners as a sponsor for us and get some new equipment!" They sure didn't see this response coming, but the laughter broke the tension. So did the fact that I didn't disagree, but accepted their evaluation as well as acknowledged their honest opinion. It was then my turn to be honest.

"Look, I can't make you a great band. I can't. I'm sorry if you think that's why I was hired. I'm just not that guy. But I'll tell you this: I can show you how to be a great band, and then it's up to you. Now, before you decide whether you want to stay in or leave, there's something else I want to tell you. I think you're heroes. I do. I think you have an enormous amount of guts to stay in this band. I'm not sure I would have, if given the same situation. But, so far, you're here. And I think the reason you're here is because regardless of your friends, both in this group and out, regardless of what other interests you may have, or what else you think is important, you chose to stay in this group because music is that important to you. Making music is that important to you. More important than what your friends think at the very least. That says a lot to me. And I want to make music with people who have that kind of belief."

There were smiles. There was agreement, and together we plotted our goals, objectives, and strategies. Now, we were truly off and running.

We set about the task of reimaging the high school band by means of the current performance opportunities, i.e. football games. We had to be able to accomplish two recognizable major feats: play both a recognizable national anthem and school fight song. With seven performers. Outdoors. I set expectation in part by reminding the band that if the problem is that they don't play well, then the goal is to play better. I then went on to explain a basic tenet of music performance. Simply, "The better we play, the more opportunities we'll get." I wanted to give the musicians a "real-life" experience by placing them outside of academic situations where they were either recognized for good playing and performance, or not.

The onus, then, was on us to practice, rehearse, and prepare for each performance to the utmost of our capabilities. Still, seven wasn't a large performing ensemble when the venue was a football field. The answer to that challenge could be found every weeknight on the *David Letterman Show* via Paul Shaffer and "The World's Most Dangerous Band." A keyboard-driven musical unit with amplified winds. Perfect. I owned a Roland D-50 programmable keyboard at the time that could not only sequence entire background parts for my band, but that also contained various percussion samples that would enable me to add the percussion parts separately as needed! Yep, we could have "We Will Rock You."

I would, however, need a leap of faith for the other part of this solution. I needed a professional sound system that was not only durable, but provided the capability to run a keyboard, four microphones, and whatever else I might want to run through it. The principal was unable to provide the two thousand dollars needed to fund such a system, but the boosters were ready, willing, and able. In a win-win scenario, the purchase also provided a sound system for school events and guest speakers. The principal was delighted in this solution. I knew that this also might help future band considerations, too. Although we had eliminated the problem of band numbers and volume, we had also upped the ante in terms of performance expectation. If someone made a mistake now, it would be painfully obvious. It was woodshed time.

With the goal of generating student interest and raising expectation, it took us three weeks before we finally had a presentable SSB and school fight song. We even had a couple of thirty-second time-out tunes, too. It would take us the rest of the semester to learn more of those time-out tunes and only one full-length song. Concert music was still out of the question, but I began to work chamber music in via interchangeable collections. Of course, everything we played was, in effect, chamber music, but I knew that core musicianship and music of more artistic merit had to be addressed in order to move students toward broader musical goals.

During this first semester, things started to change. The band was, well, rocking! Parents, teachers, and the community were responding extremely well to a new and better-sounding band. The student body was responding as well. Even referees at football games would come up and tell the band members how great they sounded. In turn, as the cycle goes, the band practiced more, rehearsed harder, and began to believe in their abilities.

Then other things began to follow suit, much like I mentioned to the band they might. We were invited to play for the local small college football team, which led to a regular gig as that same school's pep band during basketball season. Talk about a source of pride, these high school musicians providing music for a *college* event. Of course, the dance routines by the college girls at halftimes provided an interesting education as well.

During that first fall came an opportunity to perform for a minor league soccer game. While that may not seem like much, three thousand spectators were more than any of the students had performed in front of before. They stood at the center of the field, single microphone in front of them, and played the national anthem, the one piece I told them could open doors to some cool experiences. Three thousand spectators screamed their approval. Seven band students had never felt prouder. Another soccer game followed, a hockey game, then local performances for the Kiwanis and Lions clubs in which we strung our thirty-second timeout tunes into a medley that included some humor and an explanation of our program. Then, an opportunity came out of the blue that would have an enormous impact on the program, as well as sending a statement about performance quality.

The new governor-elect was from our town. He happened to be a graduate of the local college where we had performed. Word had gotten to his "people" about this little, local high school band with the big sound and energy. When I received the call, I was excited and petrified. We had just been invited to perform as part of the governor's inauguration activities at the state capitol. More specifically, we had been invited to perform inside the rotunda on the day of the inauguration—the only band to have ever been invited to do so. I spoke with the principal. I spoke with the boosters. Everyone was supportive. Next, I put it before the band. They thought I was joking. I assured them I was not. I also assured them that we would need full-length charts because thirty-second timeout tunes would get a little tedious when trying to fill out a thirty-minute program. And we had one month to do it, not an entire semester.

They accepted the challenge.

Our development of a higher performance standard had not only created opportunities; it had now forced the band into raising their level of performance expectation even higher. They were starting to become a, well, *normal* band, capable of *normal* expectations, like playing entire pep band tunes.

By the time we arrived at the statehouse for the special day, the students were as prepared as they could be. We went through the security check, set up our equipment, and toured the building. What an experience for our students to see where the governance of the state emanated from. At the designated time, we returned to the performance site in the enormous and beautiful rotunda and waited patiently for our performance time, which was to be one of the last things to occur before the swearing-in ceremonies for the state officials. Before we knew it, we were given the official okay and we lit that place up like a bonfire doused in gasoline. It was groove city. From "Mony, Mony" to "Gimme Some Lovin'" to "Land of a Thousand Dances," the band brought it. The packed rotunda yelled, swayed, and cheered. I didn't even notice the tap on the shoulder at first. The second time I brushed it off. The third time I whirled around to confront this person who was interrupting, only to stare right into the eyes of the governor-elect, holding his very young daughter in his arms. I apologized, congratulated him, and thanked him for the honor of having us perform. I then asked if he wanted to make gubernatorial history. With that, we launched into the "Hey Song," led by none other than the future leader of the state.

From there it was a blur. The musicians were instant celebrities back home. The recognition, the pride, the sense of accomplishment, everything was in the right direction. But I still knew that we weren't where we needed to be with regard to the educational mission. The "repertoire" that we had been working on wasn't listed in Acton Ostling's study regarding wind band music of serious artistic merit, let alone Jay Gilbert's update of it, and probably not revisions being prepared by aspiring doctoral students, either. But I also had learned that you have to meet the students where they are in order to take them where you want them to be.

I remember doing a clinic about repertoire and blasting arrangements that had come out. One of them was a concert band arrangement of Outkasts's "Hey Ya." Thought it was the most stupid thing I

had ever heard. C'mon, southern rap/hip-hop for concert band? After
the clinic I had a very kind gentleman come up to me and take issue
with not only a bit of the clinic, but that tune specifically. He explained
to me that he had tried to get his musicians to look at more "serious"
music, but was unable to. The program he had inherited was a wreck
and trying to keep kids in band, let alone recruit more, was a formi-
dable challenge. What he chose to do was program something he knew
his young musicians listened to: rap and hip-hop. Enter "Hey Ya." The
students had laughed at first because the arrangement sure didn't sound
like the original, but the melody was unmistakable. They liked it. They
liked it and wanted to play it all the time, which allowed this brilliant
educator a chance to work musical concepts as well as basic balance,
blend, and intonation. The band got better and, as they got better, the
teacher challenged them to music written specifically for band. Since
they had now grown both receptive and hungry for more knowledge,
he also exposed them to recordings and live concerts. I understood his
point. He used what they knew to teach what they didn't know. He
opened their minds to a whole new world by not squelching the place
they currently called "home." And that's where I was now. The students
had progressed with repertoire that was easily recognizable and accessible, but now it was time to work on rep with a bit more substance.

We continued to perform in and around our home town, local
celebrities that we were, but we also began to really focus on the chamber literature that we were doing. I was able to get a few of the students
to participate in the spring regional solo/ensemble festival and one
even made it to state. We featured our chamber groups—trios, duets,
and soloists—on our spring concert. We began listening to recordings
and looking at concert band repertoire in order to see what else was

out there. We also had a formal curriculum established, which required the students to play scales, rhythms, and excerpts appropriate to their experience. We were gaining momentum.

The next year our numbers climbed a bit, from seven to twenty-one musicians. I continued the same path, but knew that I would need a real paradigm shifter to make things happen. I needed an outside experience that would in some way drive our numbers, our support, and our musical mission. Remember: I still had absolutely no concert percussion and very little of the instruments needed for a full concert band. The band had not been on a trip in years. I wanted to find a trip opportunity that would encompass the three areas found in most traditional programs: concert, jazz, and marching bands. Now, along with no percussion, we had no piano, drum set, or guitar amplifier. Of course, we had no concert, jazz, or marching bands, either. I believed, though, we would have.

The third year was my goal to really bring the program into complete existence. I knew that bowl games often contained festivals. My school was football oriented and the "prestige" of being involved in some way with a bowl game would be understood. We made a recording with our band of twenty-one, which contained our hits from our version of the "most dangerous band." No concert music, no jazz music, and certainly no marching band; just an example of what we currently did and a portfolio of recommendation letters from various performances. While I knew that some bowl games were user-friendly, I didn't know how far the "friendly" part went. Small is small. I focused on one bowl game that was fairly close and that carried some pretty serious name equity in our area. The Cotton Bowl would make us or break us.

When it was decided that we weren't too small, and that we could, indeed, attend an event that welcomed bands our size, I approached the administration with the invitation. I had already discussed what I was going to try and do, but I don't think that it was perceived as being possible, given the history of the program. The principal, an ex-football player and tremendous supporter, leaned forward on his desk, put his weight on his elbows, and stared in disbelief. To ease his shock I discussed cost per student, timelines, and perhaps most important, that we were going to be entering a festival and competing in divisions for which we currently had no ensembles! In retrospect, that didn't ease his shock much. I asked him to let me run with this, ensuring I would make it happen.

The next meeting was with the music booster executive board. After their initial shock, they jumped right to planning fundraisers. I then reminded them that this puppy was going to be a bit more challenging because we weren't simply raising funds for students and fees; we also had to figure out a way to equip our band program to support a full concert band, jazz ensemble, and a marching parade band. They were undaunted. I was relieved. The idea seemed to be taking flight. Now it was time to ready for the addition of a parade band, a jazz ensemble, and, most importantly, a concert band to the high school curriculum!

The previous school year I had given my principal a three-year projection to give him an idea of what to possibly expect with regard to instrumental and other equipment needs for the growth of the band. Because of the band's recent history I also assured him I would ask for nothing if it were not driven by real need, i.e. we have a student, but no instrument. I had also done my research to project that it was this year, my third year in the program, that I felt I might have a chance to expand the program into a more comprehensive one. The exposure of the band through various local and regional performances as well as the governor's inauguration and the perception that the quality of the band had rapidly improved had all seemed to do the trick.

We began that third year with thirty-three members, up from the twenty-one the previous year and the seven we started with. Most important, our retention was outstanding and the instrument switches I had encouraged students to try were paying off. Those thirty-three high school band members included a bassoonist, an additional horn player, a baritone player, and a tuba player! We now had enough basic instrumentation in each section to perform appropriate literature as well as start a jazz ensemble. Now we had four months to deal with football and basketball season while establishing the basics of a concert band, jazz band, and learning to march well enough to form a parade unit before the big bowl game. Oh, yes, and raise the funds needed while still trying to get the instruments needed. Thankfully, the instrument challenge was already being met.

At every opportunity the previous year I explained our situation to anyone and everyone who would listen. School performances, community performances, talks, even chance meetings in the grocery store. I was both amazed and humbled at the response. At our spring concert the previous semester, as I stood on rickety risers, I announced that the band had been accepted to perform at the bowl game. I explained our plans to expand the program, hopefully capturing the opportunity for these students what their parents had experienced twenty years prior when they were here and the program was recognized statewide.

I then explained the challenge of instrumentation. I didn't ask for anything; I just wanted to spread awareness of the need. Two parents met me immediately afterward and not only designated the instruments they wanted to purchase for the program, but provided the check! And it never stopped. In the course of one year, forty thousand dollars was raised to outfit the band program with all of the instruments necessary to not simply compete but to provide musicians with the tools to learn about music, to make music, and to love music. The funds came largely by means of private donation with assistance by the music boosters. It seemed all I had to do was simply announce what instrument we might require and the money would appear.

The power of belief in music, in the importance of music and what it can provide, and the source of pride the school community had in its band program was absolutely humbling. This school's population was simply waiting to believe in the power of strong musical arts and the impact it could have not just in the school, but the community at large. We had everything we needed. Everything. And now it was the student's turn. What would they do with the tools they had? They answered that loud and clear.

The high school concert band, bolstered by the experience of the incoming freshman from the middle school band that was no longer marching, quickly took to pursuing the concert band concept. In fact, they were hungry for a deeper musical experience (thankfully). They followed suit with the jazz ensemble, too. Although reluctant, they understood that the parade band was an important experience and exposure to it might lend itself to additional opportunities in college. We had sectionals, private lessons, and an occasional rehearsal. I vowed that I would spend as little extra time rehearsing as possible, although the jazz ensemble met as an extracurricular activity already. I wanted the students to understand that it was quality of rehearsal, not quantity, that would adequately prepare them. I also knew that one hundred percent of the band was already involved in at least one school team or club and that sixty-six percent of those were in two or more.

I refused to consume their lives. I knew that eventually they would happily realize that music does this, all on its own. But we had fun along the way. Because the band had recently had such a horrible reputation, I couldn't help but have a little fun at the expense of some of my area colleagues. One of the two flagship universities in our state had a director of bands known as widely for his dedication to music and music education as well as for his sense of humor. I had asked him if he wouldn't mind giving the band a clinic on a rare Saturday morning. In the fall. After their marching band banquet. I told him that I certainly understood if he was unable to accept the invitation because of his schedule. The university's marching band was both a tremendous source of pride for the university and a wonderful model for music educators and their celebration would probably take awhile, most likely running very, very late the evening prior to our clinic.

Well, he accepted and the trap was set. Sure enough, he showed up with his assistant director, appearing a little tired and glassy-eyed. I escorted them to our "bandeteria" and showed them to their seats. Once they were settled, I asked our celebrity clinician what he would like us to do.

"Why don't you just play through the program?" he said.

"Perfect," I responded. I gave the band the nod. It was on. A lot of parents had gathered to watch the rehearsal and were seated in the bandeteria, giving us a solid little audience with our guest of honor seated front and center. I raised my baton and waited for that dramatic pause. I then gave a beautiful, legato, *piano* preparation, followed by a most delicate down beat. And Pandora's box opened. The band launched into a loud obnoxious, improvised version of "Louie, Louie," in a couple of keys, out of tune, out of time with each other, and as loud as they could play. Witnesses would later say they saw our guest give a rather large jolt, despite his head still hanging slightly to the right.

We played through one chorus and stopped. We acted as though it was the best we had ever played, and the band and I peered at this poor, tired, traumatized, wonderful educator and awaited his response, his wisdom, and his acknowledgement. The silence that followed was interminable. The parents didn't know what was going on either, which only added to the drama. You could feel the tension. Finally, our clinician uttered, "Ummm. Well . . . " I suggested we try it again and before he could answer, we began our "real" first piece. We lasted about sixteen measures before stopping. It was clear he had been had. The band absolutely fell out. Our guest made a reference to my parental status at birth and the entire room, breathing a sigh of relief, broke into hysterics. By this point, several of the older kids in the band were in tears, partly from laughing and seeing our guest's reaction for sure, but also for a deeper realization and discovery. In that moment, through that little musical joke, they realized they had "arrived." They were credible. "Louie, Louie" was how the old band had actually sounded . . . on a good day. Their music making was now taken seriously. The band was confident, as prepared as they knew how to be and truly excited for the big bowl trip.

As the trip approached, final payments, instructions, and rehearsals filled the time. The concert band was ready to take their knocks at their first formal festival with a "national" judging panel. The full jazz ensemble, which included seven students willing to improvise for the first time in public, the parade unit, and the concert band were ready to be evaluated from a "nationally recognized panel." From the beginning, we discussed that this was an opportunity to get feedback from very different perspectives. I explained that music competitions were simply a tool, a barometer of sorts, provided by objective experts who could provide honest evaluation of what they heard. And finally, I told them, no matter how bloody it might get, that's how you get better. Any competition is really about competing against our own standard. How anxious were they to take their knocks? They asked if they could move up a division to "compete" with larger schools with what they perceived might be a higher expectation. So that's what we did.

As luck would have it, the normally warm southern climate in Dallas that late December/early January was rocked with the first snowstorm in years, followed by ice. Our first event was the bowl parade. We filed out of the bus (we only needed one), dressed to the hilt, preparing for the cold. We warmed up and proceeded to the staging area as snowflakes the size of nickels began to fall. As we were waiting, who should walk up? The target of our "Louie, Louie" prank. His university's football team had been selected for that bowl game, so his outstanding band was there. And he took the time to find us. That gesture spoke volumes. The kids were so appreciative. He jokingly asked what we were playing on the parade route.

We survived the snow parade and after a long day of waiting, marching, waiting, and shivering, we boarded the bus to attend the massed band rehearsal. The massed band is normally a non-marching affair where, generally, as many musicians as will fit are crammed onto a football field where they all stand and perform the same music, hopefully at the same time . . . if all goes well. If it does, it can be pretty cool for all involved except the conductors who lose both weight and years off their lives worrying that it won't. Our students had been preparing their parts, but they still weren't ready for that mass of humanity on an indoor field. The size of the massed band easily quadrupled our school's student population. There was a quick explanation and then more than four hundred musicians began to play. And the volume of sound . . . what an experience for our students.

The next day was the day we had really been looking forward to. Our concert band and jazz ensemble would be performing in a festival for the first time. In my mind we had finally turned a corner. We had a band *program*, anchored by our concert band. The concerts themselves seemed to just fly by. The musicians performed at their ability and seemed unfazed by the festival proceedings, just being excited to be able to play music together and enjoy the experience. We gathered after each performance, discussing what we felt went right and what we needed to do to improve. We left it at that, excited about the football game and massed-band spectacle that we were to be a part of. And of course, cheer for our "local" football team. With that, we were off to the last mass rehearsal, with awards to follow.

To be honest, I still can't remember when exactly the awards were presented. I just know they were, because a strange thing happened. Strange, indeed. The drum majors or a representative from the bands were to line up for the presentation of awards. We took a quick poll of anyone who might like to represent us, which would involve standing, waiting, and congratulating those schools who received awards, in some cases supposedly validating the outstanding instruction they received and the expertise with which they performed . . . By default, it was decided that our drum majors would do the honors. I told them to walk up, be professional, and be sure to congratulate the other schools. All seemed to be in order until the awards for our division were presented; it was announced that our marching band had placed third. Now, the chaperones understood placing. The students weren't quite sure what had just happened. The drum majors without question weren't sure what to do, but they had been observant! One of them stepped out, shook the hand of the presenter, and stepped back; we didn't really do salutes at our school. During this process, the parents excitedly explained to the students what had just happened.

Next, the jazz awards. Thankfully, we didn't hear our school mentioned in our division.

At least until they announced first place.

This time the band went into shock. The members of our jazz band were very, very quiet. Then our lead trumpet was recognized as the outstanding jazz soloist for the festival. Our group's cheers rocked the place. I couldn't have been prouder as this young man's fellow musicians mobbed him out of respect, support, and love. By now, it was getting a little much.

And then it happened a third time. Our little thirty-three-member concert band was announced in first place in our division—the "higher" one they wanted to be in. Our "marching band" had received a "II" rating and the jazz and concert groups had received straight "I" ratings. The best thing: Nobody cared. Sure, they were excited that they had done so well, but it wasn't just about the awards; they understood the larger journey that this had been. They understood that the music mattered above all, more than anything they did to prepare for the trip and the competition. It was the music that mattered. Those trophies? They had a plan for those.

The game and half-time experiences the next day were unbelievable for the musicians. They had never performed for that many people, although those experiences in doing the SSB at so many minor league events helped put the students at ease. It also helped that out of the hundreds of students participating, our students got serious screen time on the "giant score board," probably because we didn't wear standard uniforms. We figured bands were louder with instruments and since music was the emphasis, we chose to purchase instruments instead of focusing on our "visual" program. We created a uniform style that worked for both athletic and concert events, was of minimal cost, still looked great, and instantly established a recognizable image. It truly is amazing what you can do with a white tux shirt, bowtie, cummerbund, marching pants, and a white fedora.

At the conclusion of the Bowl, we piled on the bus, exhausted from the experience. As we headed out of town, I remarked to the students how proud I was of them. They represented themselves, the band, the school, and the state well. I thanked them for all their hard work, but left unsaid the greater accomplishment they had made. I knew and they knew that music had made a difference in their lives, that music bonded them, that music had created this experience for them

On the way back, the newspaper called to interview students for a front-page article. A police escort waited for them as we neared the city limits. Normally, the only students at this school who got this kind of attention were the outstanding athletes. Regional and state championship teams had gotten used to this, but for musicians, this was entirely new. The students took it in stride, enjoying the attention, but wanting to go home and sleep.

It was custom to place any trophy that an athletic team had won on the main counter in the office for all to see for at least a week. The counter was constantly covered with trophies representing football, basketball, golf, softball, baseball, and volleyball. But on that Monday after holiday break, three music trophies and a plaque adorned the counter. They remained there by request for two weeks. After that, they went back to the music room, where they were promptly placed into a cardboard, toilet roll box and thrown on top of an old percussion cabinet, out of sight by the students. They decided they didn't need those trophies to validate who or what they were. They knew. They knew what music had done for them and they each knew the importance it had in their lives and how it fit in their lives. The trophies would stay in that box because they discovered that the musical moments and the journey they had all taken together was what truly mattered. Oh yes, they had discovered one more thing:

They didn't "suck" anymore.

It would seem that this little tale would be a bit self-serving, but it truly isn't. It is an example of synergy, of the possibilities that music can bring both in and out of the classroom in a way which affects not only students, but also parents, the school, the community, and the director himself. Specifically, I believe a key element in the resurgence of this program was the musical experiences of the parents. Parents supported us because, they too, had been involved in instrumental music as kids themselves, and they recognized that this experience continued to shape them, both musically and in other ways. Yes, as a responsible music educator I had done my homework. Yes, I had established an informed direction. Yes, I had established a musical standard. Any of us would and should in such a situation. However, the meteoric expansion of the program, its support, and its funding, was in large part a result of the support of parents and others in the community whose own lives had been touched by music in a meaningful way. They now chose to give back.

Changing a musical culture takes time, but discovering one that already exists can have immediate impact. Perhaps, when we look at the lawmakers and decision makers at local, state, and national levels, we might think about that very thing. Do we really need to prove the importance of music in our lives? Or, possibly, should we be seeking to tap into a resource that may already be found in each person, including those in positions of power? Feeling has always been more powerful than talking. Maybe that's a concept that could be utilized better. I know those seven original members stayed through thin and then thick because of how they felt about music. Perhaps your musicians are yearning as these did. Now, if we build it . . .

SIGNPOSTS

What:

Building or reorganizing a program: the basics.

When:

The year or summer prior to the anticipated change.

How:

1. Plan your work, then work your plan. Begin with what you want your program outcomes to be. In other words, where are you going?

2. Do the research. Understand the history of the following: program, school, city/town, area, previous directors, and demographic. Demographic is important if for no other reason than it's tough to build a program or following if the community is gradually aging/retiring or is turning into a bedroom community. Make note of key organizations and businesses and those who lead them. These could be potential supporters.

3. Construct "The Plan." It should include:
    - Mission Statement (Tie in with your school or organization)
    - Purpose Statement (Tie in with your school or organization)
    - Outcome Statement (Tie-in with your school or organization)
    - How you intend to accomplish the above ("The Plan")
    - Timeline for success
    - Current weaknesses:
    - Current strengths:

4. Establish a curriculum! This is the educational foundation for "The Plan!"

5. Run everything by your administration first. By doing this you do two things. You ensure that what you're doing is understood by those who may be your first line of defense with parents, enabling them to speak to what you're doing. And, you make sure that the language is appropriate.

6. Things to remember:
    - Teach belief in the program through the pursuit of quality music making.

- Esteem, awareness, and honesty are key.
- Think "quality," not "quantity."
- Small things done *well*.
- Repertoire is crucial!
- Chamber groups develop individual musicianship in extraordinary ways.
- Provide musical exposure via recordings, live performances, YouTube ...
- Bring in guest conductors and artists.
- Be sure to focus on school awareness and administrative support.
- Always know "The Star Spangled Banner" and the school fight song ...
- Discuss with members both the importance of and how to portray a positive image when in view of others.
- Expect 120 percent.
- Establish mentor programs:
- Train student coaches.
- Join a local Tri-M chapter.
- Establish community outreach programs, i.e. playing in nursing homes or for community organizations.
- The tone is set in the first two to three years. Your program's musical and educational standards are then established.
- Get feedback!
- Parents are a tremendous source of support, network opportunities, finance, and creativity.
- Administration can't support you if they don't know what you're doing. Always keep them in the loop and informed *before* that problem may arise.

- Colleagues and mentors can offer a tremendous amount of ideas, insight, and support. You don't have to do anything alone.
- Students are the bottom line and driving force. Always ask yourself, "What's best for *them* regarding their musical experience?"

For Love of Music

I
t is twenty degrees with a slight wind. There are just a few random, small flakes of snow falling. The air is clean and fresh. Surrounding me are beautiful aspen and coniferous trees, just like in those postcards. The snow is deep, but this path is at least visible. I am wearing what I normally do when I'm running in cold weather, except I'm not running: I'm snowshoeing.

For the first time in my life.

I'm strapped into snowshoes and couldn't be giddier as I walk across the snow. I quickly find out that my windproof, cold weather running pants have a drawback, as the backs of the snowshoes flick snow down my uncovered boot tops, melting, then freezing into chunks of ice between the back of the boots and my ankles. But I don't care. I am having a blast—me, along with four university students and the band director who brought me to the Michigan Upper Peninsula, or the "U.P.," as it seems to have always been referred to in reference to the two land masses that make up the state of Michigan.

The U.P. locals refer to themselves as "yoopers." You can even buy a "Yooperman" t-shirt at the Lunch Bag on Sheldon Street. My motel in Houghton was swollen with weekend tourists on snowmobiles. Some took their chances riding the canal, but most followed the myriad of trails leading out of town. They were everywhere this middle part of February, the drone of high-performance engines sounded like a giant swarm of bees on a bad day. At the gas station, outside restaurants, parked beside the motel, you couldn't look much anywhere and not see a snowmobile. Ski slopes rose across the canal, visible out of the lobby window of my motel. The skiers looked like ants sliding down a scoop of vanilla ice cream.

Before the summer tourists and the onslaught of weekenders, the U.P.'s economic backbone was mining and this beautiful northern Michigan peninsula is proud of its mining heritage. The dialect of the locals is quite distinct, in part traceable to the Finnish, who first took this area as their own. The people are warm, kind, quick to laugh, and tough. You have to be when you get over two hundred fifty inches of snowfall a year and you're lucky to have four months completely snow-free. It was logical, then, that mining pushed the technological advances here and that a local technical college was established, now boasting about seven thousand undergraduate and one thousand graduate students. These, however, ain't your average students. Houghton is a Mecca, of sorts, for engineering students of various disciplines. And, as one might expect, they're smart. Way smart. Super-Yooper smart.

Something of interest here: You may have noticed no mention of music at this university. Well, that's why we have a story. Michigan Tech doesn't offer a major in music, but they do have a music program which includes choirs, concert bands, jazz bands, an orchestra and the Huskies Pep Band. Every aspect of their music program exists to contribute to the local culture and to provide students in, say, biochemistry, molecular biology, chemical and mechanical engineering, or secondary education the opportunity to continue to do something simply because they love it: make music. The Huskies Pep Band, whose members wear black and gold striped overalls along with the band hockey jersey, is legendary in these parts. The jazz band is terrific and the Superior Wind Symphony (with its balanced instrumentation including two oboes—one doubling on English horn, two bassoons, two bass clarinets, contra-bass clarinet, and four horns) was the reason I was there. And there, at that moment, meant hiking, climbing, and sliding the Hungarian Falls the afternoon prior to our evening concert.

As I moved along that white, bumpy carpet, a lot of things came to mind. I thought about where I was at this time and place, and what got me there. I had to be careful, though, because things were starting to get a bit more technical with our little outing. Chris, one of the students, pointed to a small waterfall, hidden by the snow. I watch as he descended a small gulley, followed by Nick, Mike, and then Jake. Jake was wearing a pair of homemade snowshoes, fashioned out of the side-walls of an old set of 225/60 R-16 tires, with webbing riveted to create both traction and provide a means to strap his shoes in. Of course, they worked wonderfully. Those engineering students . . . Michelle took the high path around the falls. I, loving a challenge, began to descend the small gulley. After thinking too much and trying to read the terrain like a puzzle, I just went—stepping straight into the gulley.

Those fifteen feet down become a path of honor for my snowshoeing prowess.

Until I slipped and fell on my backside. Pride cometh . . . But the short descent was worth it and only the beginning. We trekked on, now following a stream. It was frozen on top, but water still moved underneath. At times it was difficult to tell what was solid ground and what was frozen stream because of the snow cover—except I learned that solid ground didn't crack and wasn't wet underneath. The next set of frozen, twenty-five-foot falls was even more spectacular. I noticed, though, that we were going to have to go up to get out. I started to climb, but I kept slipping. I just couldn't seem to get up! And it was during that short, thirty-foot ascent that Michelle gave me a lesson that I will always remember: Put your weight on your toes when you go up hill. Don't go back on your heels. I almost rocketed up the hill as I pondered the lesson.

The hike/climb began to become surreal. Beautiful. Breathtaking. And it was right then that I realized that it was love that brought me here. Love of music, of art, of craft, by students who weren't required to do so. They embraced it because they needed it and they loved making music with others. They embraced it because it was important to who and what they were. They embraced it because, somewhere in their life, it had embraced them.

We were hiking along a ridge now, when Chris, who knew these trails best, gave us the option, again, of the easy way or the hard way. I learned long ago that the hard way often has the most reward, so, again, I didn't answer his query, but simply took off. This one, though, was steep. Steep, steep. Chris began first, sliding, followed by Mike, then me. I really didn't appreciate the length of descent until I was able to start it and truly see, for the first time, how long and challenging it was. I've been on playground slides that had exponentially less incline than this. This was the kind of descent that conjured up all those visions of movies where people slide off the mountain to their death, except that here, there was nothing to slide off of, just into: trees. But, of course, the trees weren't close enough together to allow you to use them for support. And, to make matters worse, the descent was at least a good fifty to seventy-five yards.

As I took my first few steps, I watched as first Chris, then Mike, took scary, unplanned long slides before being able to catch themselves. At this point, I was thinking about my wife, kids, job, mortgage, insurance . . . you get the picture. I was also trying not to remind myself that everyone in our little party is no more than half my age—except the band director, who isn't much over half. Aw, so what. What an opportunity! What a challenge! Heck, I've tackled Persichetti, Holst, Stravinsky, Schwantner, and a myriad of others, not to mention surviving the entire doctoral process. Besides, it ain't like I was looking at the Berg *Kommerconcert* here. So I went on.

The first thing I realized was that I had to keep these snowshoes, with their claws, in front of me. The second thing was to keep my center of balance low. All it would take would be a shoe getting caught on this descent and I'd blow a knee out or snap an ankle. And I had a concert that night! Everything started okay, then, about halfway down, it happened. The snow just gave way a bit under me, and I slid straight down on my running pants and jacket. By the way, Spandex can really slide. I did all I could to keep the shoes in front of me and dig in, as well as digging my hands in the snow to slow me. I zoomed past Mike on my right and I saw Chris's eyes getting big. But at the same time, I let go of fear and enjoyed this incredible ride. Besides, I knew at some point something would stop me, like a tree. Ain't experience grand?

And I did stop.

The claws caught something solid. And, wouldn't you know it, I was only about twenty feet from the bottom of the gulley. When a door closes, a window opens. As I walked out a bit from the descent, I looked to my left to find Chris and Mike (Nick, Jake, and Michelle were still working their way down). And there it was. And it was yooper amazing. The falls were frozen above me at about the same height as the length of the descent I just worked down. Chris and Mike were already working their way up, very slowly. It was beautiful and I knew I had to see this thing up close. So, up I went. I discovered, quite soon, that I wasn't climbing up snow, but snow-covered ice. This was going to be tough.

As quickly as I began, I just slide back. Then, I remembered Michelle's words: weight on your toes. When you go up hill, get your weight forward on your toes to help move you forward. You put your weight back on your heels and you either sit down, slide down, or fall down. I did it and started to move slowly up. Glancing up, I noticed that Chris and Mike had eventually made it, sitting at a little cathedral opening formed by the frozen curtain of water. I was going to sit there, too. And I did, after a slow, careful ten minutes of climbing that seemed like hours. And the view and sense of accomplishment were both wonderful. I still remember looking down that frozen cascade and thinking, "Gee, that looks kind of dangerous, but I did it!" And I realized that part of the reason for my excitement was achieving something that I truly felt was, possibly, beyond what I could physically do. But with the support of others, and because of others, I had not only done it; I had learned a little more about myself, about others, about love, about music, and about the needs of the human soul.

We often times talk about feeding the soul—how important it is to continually provide the musical/artistic food that it feeds on and keeps it—and us—happy and healthy. This is something that is often one of the biggest challenges of the music profession, especially for those in music education. It can become entirely lost as we go through the day-to-day experience of working with the musicians in our charge, or in many cases replaced by the drug of music competition. However, maybe, just maybe, we've got it wrong. I was told once that nature finds a way—that no matter how urban an environment is, nature finds a way to survive. Bird nests in bank buildings, raccoons in the sewers, even that weed that finds its way through a crack in the sidewalk. Perhaps the human soul is the same. While we certainly have to feed it, I think that it, too, struggles for life. The challenge, then, is not just hearing it, but listening to it, then giving over to it. Maybe it knows what it needs. Maybe it doesn't. Maybe it just *is*. But whatever it may be, I think I briefly touched the answer snowshoeing the Hungarian Falls with five other souls, brought together simply by the love of music.

SIGNPOSTS

What:

Michelle's lesson: Put your weight on your toes! Learning to be proactive as well as creating the kind of person you want to be.

When:

Today!

How:

1. Take a moment to reflect on what is happening in your life right now. This reflection can be as narrow or as broad as

you would wish. It might pertain to working with an individual, an ensemble, learning a score, setting a new musical or educational program direction, or deciding on a career path. It might also pertain to getting through a particularly difficult time with regard to any of these pursuits, or something even more personal.

2.   Write down those reflections that you may seem to have a particular reaction to: those things that trigger a sense of frustration, concern, or sense of loss as to what to do next.

3.   Pick one. Ask yourself:
   - Do I know why I'm "stuck"?
   - Do I know what to do next?
   - Am I simply "frozen" in the "snow," unable to make any kind of decision and just emotionally spent?

4.   If you answered yes to any of the above questions, it's time to put on your snowshoes and put your weight on your toes! In other words, here are some thoughts on how to become proactive about your situation. Keep in mind that chances are you already know what to do: You simply need to get the momentum forward!
   - Talk to someone you respect. Ask a mentor what they did or might do.
   - Trust your gut and make a decision. Don't worry whether or not it's the textbook answer. All bets are off when it comes to any given situation: You must trust your own experience and expertise. College is over . . .
   - Focus on the task, not the feelings. Be objective, not subjective. Sometimes it's best just to put your head

down, get the weight on your toes, and *move*. It's amazing what just a little bit of progress can either do or illuminate!

- Take the time to look back to see not only where you've come from, but to be sure you've learned the lesson that the path taught you. In other words, is it avoidable in the future or do you now know what might help you in the event you find yourself on your heels again . . .

WHAT ARE WE REALLY DOING?

One of my favorite thought-provokers for students is an article entitled "Against Interpretation" by Susan Sontag. For those who don't recognize the name, chances are you still have heard of her if you've seen the movie *Bull Durham*. Kevin Costner's character: "Crash" Davis, goes on a diatribe at one point that includes the following tender, thoughtful observation:

"Well I believe . . . the novels of Susan Sontag are self-indulgent, over-rated crap."

Well, that may or may not be, but I do believe that her essay is terrifically thought provoking. In it, Sontag states the case for not trying to interpret a piece of art for the creator, not trying to imply meaning that may or may not be there. In fact, she essentially writes that it's okay to decide for ourselves based on our own understanding of what we experience from it.

You probably already see what a slippery slope this is. Interpretation, predispositions, composer intent . . . wow. For me, this is just the beginning, because I think that this calls into question many things associated with our vocation. First and foremost: What is the importance of music for everyone?

Let me put it this way. Why do we do what we do, who really cares, and in the end, what difference does it make? Seriously. And taking things a step further, what would happen if music stopped today? Think it can't? I can count five schools within a sixty-mile radius of where I sit writing right now that have been forced to answer that question. High school music is gone in those schools. For a couple, the elementary program is gone, too. One of those schools had a small marching band that was an incredible source of pride for its small community, but it only took one board meeting to erase that. Why? Because it was music and, when it comes to learning, music is expendable. At least that's the interpretation of many administrators and school boards. And how did we get there? Well, let's look farther back. Way back. Way, way back. At the beginning.

Ogg the Caveman took stick.

Ogg the Caveman whacked stick.

Ogg the Caveman whacked stick on 2 and 4.

Ogg the Caveman began to groove, and thus the beginnings of music history.

Okay, maybe it didn't quite happen like that, but it might not be so far off. Without getting into too much detail and with apologies to my music history professors, allow me to paint a very broad picture of music history—and music's place in history—in an effort to understand the interpretation of music as expendable.

Music was originally found in two main areas of daily life: the secular and the sacred. Secular music often revolved around rituals, tradition, and history. Sacred music served to glorify the power and existence of a supreme being... or beings, depending on where you cast your vote. It carried our beliefs, hopes, and traditions before there was quill and parchment. It accompanied those things most near and dear to the human experience. And so it went through time, the arts defining cultures for centuries.

When you studied civilizations in school, chances are you looked at the culture of those civilizations. At the heart of those cultures were probably the arts and, often, it was music that carried the words, deeds, and beliefs of its people through the generations. Okay, okay, pictures told the story, too, but *music* moved our ancestors. Chalk one up to the Big Guy/Gal for creating not only the cerebellum, but also the higher functions, especially the amygdala (a center for emotion in the brain)! Composers began to experiment with new textures, gaining compositional freedom as new instruments were created and refined in the forward march of technology.

And, of course a huge turning point: Johannes Gutenberg and his invention around 1440 of the PRINTING PRESS. The aural tradition was put somewhat at ease now that things could be more easily, readily, and "permanently" preserved, but that tradition in no way ceased in its importance. Both secular and sacred music continued to flourish. We bore out our troubles, triumphs, hopes, fears, tragedies, and ecstasies: our *life*, through music. Composers continued to pursue the means of expressing the human experience through a now rapidly changing instrumental refinement bonanza. This bonanza continues today as software enables every person to be a composer. The latest compositional development has seen the elimination of electronically generated music as a fad and in return its acceptance as an important musical means of expression, though adequate notation of such remains in its infancy. Now, here we are. How's that for a romp through music history using around four hundred words? Admittedly, what is really being outlined is a short history of the musical expression of the human experience.

Looking back again at this history, it seems at some point we just simply understood and embraced that music moved us, could transport us, beyond the simplicity of, say, the Romans marching to the beat of a drummer to move faster, farther, and quicker. Music provided the soundtrack for the major events of our lives, the majority centering on activities involving other people. Weddings, funerals, parties, church services, wars, and celebrating peace: Music has always been the cable TV/cell phone/MP3 player/digital electronic what's-it of its time. Movies? We once had operas as the major social event. Church services provided opportunity to hear the latest works by some of the most important composers in history. Music became a focal point of cultural exchange for all involved. It was *the* happening. Concerts were no longer for only the six percent upper nobility.

The beginning of music in the school has become common knowledge in music education circles, so what follows is, again, an extremely brief summary. Lowell Mason and George Webb began to formalize the teaching of music with the establishment of the Boston Academy of Music in 1932. Shortly thereafter, Mason was allowed to teach music in an elementary public school setting for a year and the resulting success saw the approval of inclusion of music in all of Boston's public elementary schools. By the middle of the nineteenth century, music would become a part of all levels of Boston's public education and the city had become the music education community to which the rest of the country aspired. The curriculum was based on teaching singing and theory as well as methods of teaching the same. Normal schools, the two-year precursor to our modern "four-year" colleges and universities, would provide the needed instruction for teachers. To this point, however, we're dealing primarily with the widespread teaching of vocal music. Instrumental music as it is recognized today would enter most schools through the social backdoor: It accompanied school events and growth in the early twentieth century was substantial. This wider acceptance of instrumental music would lead to an emphasis on performance in addition to "simply" music education.

The Music Supervisor's National Conference, what we now recognize as MENC, the National Association for Music Education, was founded in 1907 in Iowa to support the rapid interest and proliferation of music programs in schools. Although now established as a bona fide curricular subject, music was still an important part of school functions, one of its primary responsibilities. It was an integral part of the school fabric and provided a source of school and community pride, as well as education. The advent of radio didn't slow things down any. Records either. In fact, live music still flourished and people still placed enormous emphasis on it. Live music was *it*. Even popular music, that *jazz* music, found its way into the school. Music represented who we were and what we did.

What we started to notice, though, was that there was something more. Music had become such an extension of us, of our schools, of our societies, that we never thought about not having it. We discovered, as Aristotle did so long ago, that music did, indeed, help balance who we were. It allowed us to create, express, and reflect. It connected us in ways that were as yet unexplained, something deep in us, an entrainment of souls. We couldn't imagine life without music. Our schools sensed this importance and placed more emphasis on the study of music, bringing most aspects of it into the regular school day rather than recognizing it in only club or extracurricular status.

Beginning in the middle of the twentieth century, seminars and organizations promoting and supporting the importance of music and music teacher education brought new focus. MENC's 1950 "The Child's Bill of Rights in Music," the 1959 Ford Foundation's " Young Composers Project," the 1965 "Seminar on Comprehensive Musicianship" at Northwestern University, the 1967 Tanglewood Symposium on a unified philosophy of music education, the 1978 Ann Arbor Symposium on learning theory in music education, and the list goes on, including, of course, MENC's 1994 National Standards for Music Education. Let's not forget the establishment of the National Orchestra Association (1930), the College Band Directors National Association (originally a committee within MENC until 1941, but under this name since 1947), the American School Band Directors Association (1953), The National Band Association (1960), the American Choral Directors Association (1961), and the myriad of other professional organizations supporting music and music teachers. Even the launching of Sputnik in 1957 and increased emphasis on math and science didn't seem to appear to slow school music too much. Music education boomed, and then beginning in the early 1970s, it started to bust. The battle for the importance of music education in schools saw its warning shots fired.

As I travel, I seek out those music educators who are either near retirement or who have retired. I have one very important question that I ask them: What was the biggest change you saw in music education during your time in the rehearsal room? At least ninety percent of them cite one particular and significant event.

Title IX, renamed the "Patsy T. Mink Equal Opportunity in Education Act" in honor of its main author, stated: "No person in the

United States shall, on the basis of sex, be excluded from participation in, be denied the benefits of, or be subjected to discrimination under any education program or activity receiving Federal financial assistance." Funny thing is, athletics wasn't even a main focus in the act. In fact, there is barely a mention, yet the most telling legacy seems to be in high school and university athletics. But without question, it had an effect on music, especially with regard to more school opportunities for young women than just music and the reapportionment of school budgets because of a sudden proliferation of women's athletic options. Simply, the act indirectly placed a very large importance on sports, both in terms of participation and funding. Well, this caused problems and in many areas, the rift between athletics and music grew into a chasm.

Problem was, it should not have been a rift to start with. Music was a curricular subject in the majority of schools in this country in 1972, while athletics was extracurricular. Technically, music could be said to be co-curricular, but then there's the problem of confusing school/ social function with actual, viable, appropriate music instruction. But the seeds were planted—music was the same as athletics. They were both considered extracurricular, with athletics at least grabbing more headlines and providing gate fees and concession revenue. It didn't help that a greater emphasis was then put upon competition among music groups, especially marching band and show choir. Now, if "our" ensemble received first place, then education must surely be happening. Now we can show a trophy to our parents and administration to prove that it's happening, thereby substantiating the importance of music.

I don't know about you, but right about now I've got the feeling I took a side road at night in the middle of nowhere and it turned to dirt just before the car died . . . but a funny thing happened on the way to the marching field. The concert hall started to go silent. Chairs were now empty. Where audiences used to come to listen to live music that provided a common sense of reflection, recognition, appreciation, and a sense of school community, there was now a void. Audiences were moving to the outdoors as well as to competitive concert halls. In addition, university ensembles begin to encourage and perform music that was, without question, intended to move the genre of serious music forward, especially in the world of wind band. In so doing, however, it seemed to leave the audience behind. But, are all these bad things? It's interpretation, isn't it? Yet, it's much, much more than that.

"No Child Left Behind" spawned an enormous emphasis on student learning deficiencies. Schools were now made responsible for all students and their levels of achievement, despite not being given the financial tools to do so. The actual act designated that music be considered core curriculum and both state and national standards were created to add cognitive oomph to music. And the research . . . Music makes you smarter. Music makes you more creative. Music provides an avenue to develop independent and creative thinking that will boost cognitive skills as well as help the United States rise to the top of the economic chain once again.

All very important and true, but what truly happened to the value and importance of *music*? What were the reasons for even teaching it in our schools? It seemed that, perhaps, in our efforts to prove the worth and importance of music, in trying to make music important and viable based on others expectations of learning ("No Child . . . "), we lost sight of what music really was and is, of what it did and does. We are putting so much emphasis on how it helps other disciplines that we seem to have lost sight of its inherent merit. School administrators and school boards have noticed too.

Now, here we are. The sky is falling and we are so understandably concerned with just keeping our programs afloat that we aren't able to form a cohesive thought, let alone a plan of action. Adding to this major challenge is that we still aren't sure what this music stuff truly is, though we do understand at a basic level that it is powerful and transformational. Perhaps, as evidenced by our history and current predicament, figuring it out isn't the key to the future. Remember Sontag: The idea is not to determine something for others, but for ourselves. So, here are some things I've determined, but it'll take some explaining.

Where I was born and raised, a train whistle is a welcome sound. If you lived in one of the small towns in Kansas, you wanted to hear that whistle. If you didn't hear the whistle, your small town was probably dying. No commerce, no trade, no jobs, no money, no people, and finally, no town. Music seems to be the train of the twenty-first century. I submit that when you remove music from the schools—especially cutting it off at the grade-school level (e.g. the roots and thereby the tree), you lose not simply a competitive or extracurricular support group: You begin to lose the school, and then the town. Now you've got bigger problems. What, you ask? Well, remember bussing? One of the biggest problems with bussing was the human factor that wasn't considered because it couldn't be factored into dollars and cents: its impact on the local community/neighborhood.

When I taught in the St. Louis area, I saw first hand the effects of bussing students to the suburbs. A mayor during that time made the astute observation that inner city St. Louis was in absolute disarray. And one of the biggest reasons: bussing. Why? Because a sense of community, of neighborhood, had been lost and this, in part, opened the door for gangs to step in to help provide that sense of community. Imagine you lived on a street where everyone attends several different schools. You don't have much in common, you don't see each other that much, and your parents are not involved in school activities because they are unable to attend evening activities in the suburbs and work. No connection. No commonality. No sense of community pride, just a patch of turf to defend. The human factor wasn't taken into account.

And now we're seeing a similar scenario in rural schools, except this time it's consolidation. Towns are dying out. People are moving away. Hard decisions are being made. But like the train whistle, when the school leaves town . . . Take away that community connection and source of pride and it's a slow death. Music? It's removal is a symbolic scapegoat for bigger problems, like poor budgeting and personal agendas. Interesting how, historically, music and the arts are what we fell back on to help us make sense of things, to help us through difficult times. Why? With music, we had each other. We had a bond. And now, what do we do? Because it doesn't have the word "mandatory" before the word "core," we cut the very thing that helped sustain us before. The facts are, music doesn't *necessarily* make us champions, music doesn't *necessarily* make us great, and music doesn't *necessarily* make us smarter. Nope. But what it does do is make us *human*. It provides us an avenue of wordless expression and connection. It gives us a link to the past and possibility toward the future. Of course, that doesn't create an economic impact so, off with music's head. Slash it, cut it, and remove the tumor. Cut our very sense of humanity in order that we can focus on getting smarter. Anybody else see the oxymoron here? Okay, maybe I'm just too close to the topic. Let me step back and provide a few objective observations from history, more specifically, the history of aggression, oppression, and the human factor involved.

The kobzari are Ukrainian minstrels who originally performed on a stringed instrument resembling a lute, although the instrument gradually took a different shape and added strings to its present day appearance. Historically, until 1939, kobzari had to be blind and received instruction by means of apprenticeship from other kobzari. Organized in church-related guilds, they were led from village to village where they performed in not only homes, but also outside churches and at religious festivals and fairs. Their repertoire was predominantly religious songs and those they performed for greatly valued these songs and what they did for their own souls. Giving the performer alms for a performance was a means of lifting spirits as well.

You'll notice that I mentioned 1939. Socialism was raging through Europe and Josef Stalin was attempting to unify the stubborn Ukraine region with his doctrine. A main point of his doctrine was a strict adherence to atheism. The kobzari, with their historically important role in the rural and spiritual life of the Ukrainian people and the hope and power their songs provided, were a stumbling block. Stalin schemed that to conquer the people, you must crush their spirit. So, in 1939, he invited all the kobzari to a national celebration honoring them and their importance to the Ukraine. Almost all attended. Almost all were assassinated. It was a major step forward in the eventual fall of the Ukraine into complete socialism. Unfortunately in this case, it appears Stalin understood the impact of music and the human factor. As an endnote, the kobzari tradition has returned, but not in quite the same context as it once originally existed. Music? Art? Impact? Here's another example, though in a bit broader context.

The Louvre. When Nazi Germany was set to invade Paris, one of Hitler's big plans was to loot the French national treasures housed there for both profit and to take into possession those things the country held most dear, thereby showing the French who was the dominate race/culture. From 1938–1939, before Hitler and his army arrived, thousands of the most treasured pieces of art were evacuated from the Louvre and distributed around the provinces. As the tale goes, every painting, statue, sculpture, and book had been taken by the people of France and hidden in their homes until the war was over with the promise of bringing them all back. And they did. Every last piece. *Everything* was returned at the end of the war because of the value those things represented to the people of France. Not because they were concerned about money, economics, or anything else. It was because that content represented *who they were.* The French appeared to understand the arts and their impact on the human factor. "Okay, fine," you say. "I still don't quite follow, but I think I get the point." Well, Let me throw one more example at you in an effort to show the impact and importance of music and its relationship with the human factor.

Unlike the previous two tales in which art defines a people, this is an example where art—specifically music—helped heal us. September 11, 2001. It all changed on that day. The United States of America was knocked to its knees in an act that suddenly thrust the States into territory that, until 8:46 a.m. (UTC-4) that day, was reserved for those "other" countries, the ones who have been dealing with terrorists, extremists, and radicals for decades and even centuries. Now, I don't want to get into a discussion about theories concerning the attack, nor religious implications. What I do want to point out is this: Music started to bring us back.

Music.

Music accompanied images of that day, from the horrific footage playing out on screens to the soundtracks behind the heroes who showed us the best in who we are. From Bach to rock, concerts were organized to help raise relief benefits for those affected, with many of the musicians donating their talents. We heard songs on the radio that dealt with the tragedy, and in so doing helped us to do the same. Music tapped a deep vein in our collective consciousness and brought us together as one tribe of man. Sting was recording a live album the day of the attack. He chose to continue the project, but opened with a different tune. "Fragile" was performed, a lesson in the futility of aggression and war. There was no applause at the conclusion of the piece, just an audience united by a singular event, drawn together by a song that seemed to encompass the feelings of that day.

Many performing artists and composers dealt with the tragedy in the only way they knew: through composition and creation. Dr. Andrew Boysen was commissioned to write a multi-movement piece that was going to deal with aspects of childhood, but instead composed a grade IV piece, "Grant Them Eternal Rest," which stunningly captures feelings surrounding the events, and the beginning of the healing process. The piece does not seek to recreate the events, but to put a musical voice to the feelings of that day, and the days after. There are very few pieces that I have performed that have had such a stunning effect on a wide audience. And why does this piece do that? It's not because it was designed to make students smarter, taller, shorter, etc. It is because it is a piece that makes us examine who we are, and emotionally where we are—even now. Andy created a piece that builds musical bridges, linking the individual souls of an audience touched by those events. Though it has no words, it has emotions that we are akin to, each in our own way. One of the most gripping elements of the piece is the audience reaction after the piece: No one wants to applaud. There is a reverence, a respect that the piece implies that reaches the audience on a very basic level and the result is that applause just does not seem appropriate. But, the audience is *unified* by the impact of the experience, despite deriving individual musical conclusions. The human factor, experienced through music. Yet, it is individual musical conclusions and the resulting interpretations that have created our current challenges.

Trying to define music for each individual is an absurd pursuit, yet we try to do just that. The marching or show choir experience reaches students, parents, administrators, and general audiences in their own way. Music in the concert hall does the same. So does music in the work place, the mall, even in the elevator. In fact, I would argue that defining music performance, music education, and musical experience is not possible. The best we can really do is define what a particular experience hopes to do or accomplish, much like the music teacher's ethics will guide them in the beneficial use of competition. Expectations, outcomes, and definitions hope to point a musical path, but in the end, the magic of music, that indefinable, aesthetic culmination must be left up to each and every person. It is in that aesthetic place, served by the cognitive rather than dictated by it, that we compose our own personal definition of not just humanity, but of ourselves. Music in the schools is an absolutely vital part of that process—all types of music. If an administrator's or school board's interpretation is that music is not of worth and is removed from the school, I submit it will have a profound effect on the school's culture and the community's culture as a whole. Why? Because of what music means to each and every person affected—their personal interpretation. And it is each and every person that, in this case, constitutes the human factor.

Here's a little math problem for your consideration. If one hundred music jobs are eliminated in this country in the next year (a conservative number) and each one of those music educators were to teach one hundred students each (again, a conservative number), then ten thousand students would not have the opportunities music provides. Ten thousand. I wonder, would we be shocked at this kind of artistic repression if it was happening in another country? I wonder how those who created the Bill of Rights would have felt about this? I wish this illustration was only an example, but it's already happening. To lose the opportunity to make music in our schools, to teach music in our schools, to hear music in our schools as part of our country's fabric and educational mission, is to destroy a portion of our country's cultural future and fabric.

That can't happen. So what do we do?

First, we need the absolute best artist/educators we have ever had. We need those with the soul of a musician and the heart of a child, willing to teach music for low pay in horrible conditions with very little support and benefits. We need those who believe in the heart, who believe that one note can make a difference, and who believe that the future of music and the human soul could very well rest in that one student sitting in the middle of the third row holding an old clarinet. We need Guerilla Teachers who are willing to teach and make music regardless of the challenges. We need Music Guerillas who openly embrace music and are willing to pressure decision-makers to keep music in the curriculum. Students, parents, administrators, professional musicians, critics, your neighbor, your doctor, your mechanic, your plumber: anyone who can play, listen, or appreciate music needs to understand that the essence of who we are and our ability to define music as much as it defines each one of us in individual terms, is truly under attack.

We can *all* be Music Guerillas. And what happens if we choose to be complacent? What if we choose to look the other way or give in to the seemingly inevitable? What will this generation's (and possibly the next one's) musical legacy be? More than ten thousand hearts may have already defined it this way: Our musical legacy will be as the generation that helped contribute to our own artistic genocide. Remember that civilizations are measured by their culture. But, that's just my interpretation.

And being a Music Guerilla? That, my friends, is the power of the human factor.

SIGNPOST

What difference can you make right now and how?

Epilogue. Composing a Life

Remember that moment I talked about at the beginning of this adventure? That moment when you knew that music was the path for you? Do you have it in your mind? Can you see it or *feel* it?

Now, ask yourself why you are doing what you do. Is this where you pictured yourself one, five, ten, or twenty years ago?

For most of us, the moment arrived with such impact that it was without question an epiphany. For others it was a slow realization after a long trek—you realized that there really is nothing else you'd rather do or be. It could have been anything from tapping your silverware on the table when you were eight years old and hearing your aunt say, "You should be a drummer," to realizing after eight years of piano lessons that you might as well make a go of it. Regardless, we are all bound by that "one thing," whatever it is for each of us.

I am humbled by opportunities to guest conduct or speak with students in clinics about their musical lives. Strangely enough, for some students, either of these can be a stretch. I find that many students have their musical lives determined for them. They don't realize that they have a choice. As an example, let's look at honor groups.

We provide opportunities for students to come together, often times with like talented others, to create an experience that will only exist for a small amount of time, then no more. We hope that this experience might generate a moment that will impact these young musicians for a lifetime. We bring in terrific, talented conductor/educators (read that as ONE person, not either/or) and impose upon them the task of building to this potential life-impacting moment. And here's where it gets interesting.

A terrific ensemble reads through the introduction and first theme. The conductor gives a release. The students are obviously well prepared and have performed flawlessly. The conductor asks, "What should the audience *feel* there?" Silence. Crickets. Dull hum of fluorescent lighting. Many are waiting for the conductor to tell them *exactly* what they are trying to convey. They have done their technical duty, now Dr./Mrs./Mr. Artsy Conductor Person is expected to tell them a story about palm trees, sand between the toes, and a sunset slowly sinking into the ocean to help illustrate what is needed musically.

I remember watching a television program in which Steven Tyler of Aerosmith talked about his reluctance to make music videos to help promote albums. He felt that videos were robbing the viewers of the wonderment of realizing their own images. It was as if feelings were being imposed on them by others. Amazing how Mr. Tyler and Maestro share the same problem: having to induce an effect because, quite possibly, we are living in a culture of soulful reaction rather than action! We don't trust ourselves enough to truly draw upon our own feelings and, instead, require that someone else tell us how to feel. Besides, it's safer and easier . . .

This isn't so far removed from how students view their musical lives. "Don't worry, you'll find yourself." Really? Is someone lost? I submit it's not about finding; it's about creating ones self. It's about composing a life. Miles Davis once was quoted as saying, "Don't play what's there. Play what's not there."

Now look at that honor group.

Look at that music video.

Look at your musicians.

Look at your life.

Compose a life. And then perform it. You've heard it: "Life is *NOT* a dress rehearsal." We get one shot. Teach'em all; let life sort'em out. And like a performance, we can adjust along the way. In a performance situation, many things can happen. In fact volumes could be written about all the things that have gone wrong in musical performances. But as all true performers know, the show must go on if it all possible. Why? Because it's not about us. It's about the composer and the audience. It's about our talent and the responsibility that comes with it. It's about finding a way to make the music speak and then adjusting to any possible performance problem that may occur.

Of course, we must be honest and accountable for those problems in order to correct them and move on. Those in our charge must understand that, too. And finding oneself? Bah. How about trying a path? Trying a phrase? Trying to help them find and evoke who *they* are. Who *we* are.

"What should the audience *feel* there?" Maybe a more important question is for the musicians to ask what they themselves feel? With so many souls and experience in an ensemble, how can we not combine all that life experience and, with the conductor's informed intuition, reach a musical accord representative of the composer's intent?

So many questions, yet, ultimately we all face three unavoidable ones. They are questions that everyone at some point must at least acknowledge, but which require some kind of resolution from those who would dedicate themselves to the musical arts:

1. Where do we come from?
2. Where are we going?
3. What are we supposed to do while we're here?

If our pen never hits our manuscript paper, we will never begin to understand. The reality is, each one of us is performing a piece in progress. Each one of our lives is performance art. Eventually, a name and date of completion will be etched in marble. Will that marble be simply a tombstone? Or will it be a monument to a masterwork, a piece worthy of core repertoire that others will analyze, build upon, and continue to value?

"What should the audience *feel*?" Maybe the answer can be found in that first moment: Remember . . .?

About the Author

MILTON ALLEN is the Associate Director of Bands and a visiting professor of music at The Ohio State University. He previously served as Director of Bands and Instrumental Division Director at Eastern Illinois University. A seventeen-year veteran of the public school rehearsal room, Milt's refreshing and practical approach to music education and conducting has made him an in-demand clinician and guest conductor throughout the United States, Canada, and the United Kingdom. From British Columbia, Canada to Glasgow, Scotland, and at conferences including the Midwest Clinic, MENC regional and national conventions, and BASBWE International Wind Festivals, his humor, passion, and experience combine to illuminate the possibilities of both music education and the live art of performance.

Active in the commissioning and recording of new wind works for both developing and experienced bands, he has collaborated with numerous composers, including Michael Sweeney, Mark Camphouse, James Bonney, Jonathan Newman, Steven Bryant, and Alex Shapiro.

Ensembles under Dr. Allen's direction have received awards at local, state, and national levels, including a Citation for Musical Excellence from the United States Congress. He is a two-time Teacher of the Year and a Kansas Teacher of the Year semifinalist. Additional honors and distinctions include five teaching and service awards from the Ohio State University School of Music, and selection as a conducting fellow for the Eastman Wind Ensemble's 40th Anniversary.

In 2008, Allen became the first civilian in the history of the United States Air Force to tour as a featured conductor, performing with the USAF Heritage of America Band.

Milt lives in Columbus, Ohio with his wife Margaret, son Benjamin, and daughter Madeline.